HOW TO
WRITE YOUR
LIFE STORY

HOW TO
WRITE YOUR
LIFE STORY

The Complete Guide to Creating a Personal Memoir

KAREN ULRICH

Reader's Digest

The Reader's Digest Association, Inc.
Pleasantville, New York/Montreal/London/Sydney

This edition published by
The Reader's Digest Association, Inc.
by arrangement with
IVY PRESS LIMITED
The Old Candlemakers
Lewes, East Sussex BN7 2NZ, U.K.
Copyright © Ivy Press Limited 2006

FOR READER'S DIGEST
U.S. Project Editor: Barbara Booth
Canadian Project Editor: Pamela Johnson
Project Designer: Jennifer R. Tokarski
Associate Art Director: George McKeon
Executive Editor, Trade Publishing: Dolores York
President & Publisher, Trade Publishing: Harold Clarke

FOR IVY PRESS
Creative Director: Peter Bridgewater
Publisher: Jason Hook
Editorial Director: Caroline Earle
Art Director: Sarah Howerd, Kevin Knight
Project Editor: Mandy Greenfield, Susie Behar
Design: Jane Lanaway
Picture Research: Katie Greenwood

Library of Congress
Cataloging-in-Publication Data
Ulrich, Karen, 1968-
  How to write your life story: the complete guide to
creating your personal memoir / Karen Ulrich.
    p.cm.
  Includes bibliographical references and index.
  ISBN 0-7621-0813-4
  1. Autobiography--Authorship. 2 Biography as a literary
  form. 3. Report writing. I. Title.

CT25.U47 2006
809'.93592--dc22   2006046463

Address any comments about
How to Write Your Life Story to:
The Reader's Digest Association, Inc.
Adult Trade Publishing
Reader's Digest Road
Pleasantville, NY 10570-7000

For more Reader's Digest products
and information, visit our website:
http://www.rd.com (in the United States)
http://www.readersdigest.ca (in Canada)
http://www.readersdigest.co.uk (in the UK)
http://www.readersdigest.com.au
(in Australia)
http://www.readersdigest.com.nz
(in New Zealand)

Printed and bound in China

1 3 5 7 9 10 8 6 4 2

Contents

Introduction

Do you have a burning desire to write but don't know where to begin or what to write about? Do your experiences deserve to be recorded? Do you want to preserve your family's life story for future generations? Do you hope to use writing to recover from a troubled past or to discover something new about yourself? If you've answered yes to any of these questions, *How to Write Your Life Story* will help you move beyond contemplation and start writing. Consider this book a toolbox, with everything you need to help you put together the story of your life.

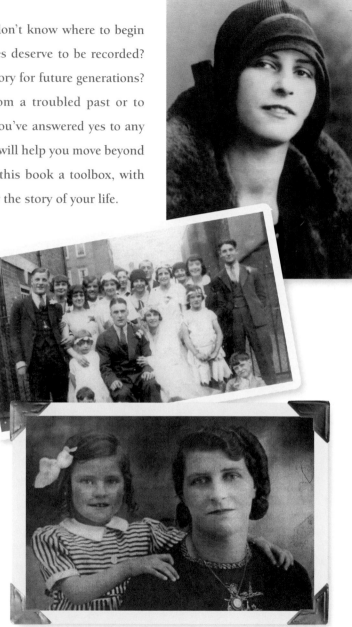

Is your story worth telling?

It used to be that only the rich or famous wrote their memoirs, and it was only these life stories that were considered important enough for publication. Fortunately for the reading public, times have changed. More and more people are choosing to recount their stories, seeking to share their experiences, frustrations, struggles, triumphs, secrets, and insights.

Given motivation and time, anyone can write a memoir—the waitress at your favorite coffee shop, the adventurer who has dedicated his life to wandering, the neighbor who has lost a child, or the accountant who wants to understand his family's history. Everyone has a story worth sharing: the trick is learning how to tell it—how to shape it on the page.

Whatever kind of project you have in mind—be it a tightly written memoir or an illustrated family scrapbook—your first task is to research and organize your material. Preparation and reflection will prove vital ingredients, combined with the discipline and effort required to follow your path of self-discovery to its end.

Whether you're a recent immigrant or have been in your country for years, nothing preserves a family's past like a family archive or scrapbook.

Fueling your imagination

Writers choose different ways to package the stories of their lives, and reading their accounts will open your eyes to the possibilities. Some writers, such as Nelson Mandela in his *Long Walk to Freedom: The Autobiography of Nelson Mandela*, opt for a chronological autobiography, documenting the entirety of their experience. Others narrow their focus to explore a specific chapter or relationship, such as Joan Didion's *Year of Magical Thinking*, which chronicles her grief following the death of her husband and the illness of her daughter. *How to Write Your Life Story* will help you select your own focus and decide what aspects of your life are most worthy of exploration.

Nelson Mandela chose to document his lifelong fight against racial oppression in his autobiography, Long Walk to Freedom. *Other writers focus on just a single event in their life.*

VOICES OF THE MASTERS

Pablo Neruda, the Chilean-born poet, argues in this excerpt from his introduction to *Confieso que he vivido: Memorias* ("Memoir: Confession I Have Lived") that the poet can use poetic license when it comes to memoir writing. For Neruda, the poet indulges in the vagueness of his memories to a greater extent than other memoir writers, who focus more on specific details.

No matter how accurate you consider your memory, you are not a movie camera, and what you remember of your life will be shaped by your emotions and your situation at that time. Realizing this can free up your writing as you develop your style.

In these memoirs or recollections there are gaps here and there, and sometimes they are also forgetful, because life is like that. Intervals of dreaming help us to stand up under days of work. Many of the things I remember have blurred as I recalled them, they have crumbled to dust, like irreparably shattered glass.

What the memoir writer remembers is not the same thing the poet remembers. He may have lived less, but he photographed much more, and he re-creates for us with special attention to detail. The poet gives us a gallery full of ghosts shaken by the fire and darkness of his time.

Perhaps I didn't live just in my self, perhaps I lived the lives of others…. My life is a life put together from all those lives: the lives of the poet.

VOICES OF THE MASTERS

Vivian Gornick, essayist and critic, explores her early life as it unfolded in relation to her mother in her celebrated memoir *Fierce Attachments*. Like Gornick's memoir, the story of your life will have its cast of characters in the same way that a work of fiction does, including you as the protagonist. An important part of memoir writing is creating a persona on the page: the narrative voice of your life story.

In the following extract from *Fierce Attachments*, Gornick muses on the unfulfilled lives, based on denial, of the women in the New York tenement where she grew up, and establishes her own persona among them, absorbing the unspoken influences they had upon her.

I lived in that tenement between the ages of six and twenty-one. There were twenty apartments, four to a floor, and all I remember is a building full of women.... They never spoke as though they knew who they were, understood the bargain they had struck with life, but they often acted as though they knew.... There would be years of apparent calm, then suddenly an outbreak of panic and wildness: two or three lives scarred (perhaps ruined), and the turmoil would subside.... And I—the girl growing in their midst, being made in their image—I absorbed them as I would chloroform on a cloth laid against my face. It has taken me thirty years to understand how much of them I understood.

A Memoir

Fierce Attachments

"One hesitates to traffic in such stock reviewer's adjectives as 'brilliant,' 'an American classic,' but there are only so many words...with which to say how very good this book is." —Susan Wood, *The Washington Post Book World*

VIVIAN GORNICK

INTRODUCTION BY JONATHAN LETHEM

Vivian Gornick, an active member of the U.S. feminist movement, began her writing career 30 years ago. The role of women in her life, and in the wider world, are subjects that are an integral part of her writing.

Deciding on a story

Your life story is, by definition, a story from your life, but beyond that it might be about anything. Perhaps your story is a coming of age, or an account of a relationship; perhaps it focuses on a personal tragedy such as the loss of a loved one or a serious illness. It might be a recount of a travel adventure or a collection of stories inspired by your career as a medical worker. Maybe it's the story of an athletic achievement, or a legal battle, or your personal take on a specific place, a particular time, or a significant event in history.

Or maybe you have no idea—you know you want to write, but don't know what you want to write about. It's not uncommon to be unaware of your story or its themes until your project is well under way. Don't worry: The exercises in this book will help you get started and guide you through to the end. As you will discover, there are many ways in which you can throw out your net for ideas. You can interview family and friends, read old journals, or focus on collecting imagery. Above all, you'll need to exercise your memory. Small writing tasks and list making are excellent ways to conduct research on your life, as you'll find out. Once your research is under way (or perhaps not until you begin writing), your story will start to take shape. You may be surprised to realize how little you know about the life you've lived. Let your inspiration guide you and keep your mind open to changes in direction.

You might wish to begin with a memory that frequently visits. Is there a specific moment, relationship, or time period that you often find your mind wandering back to? Perhaps there is an old friend whom you haven't seen in 23 years, but who

played a significant role in your development as an adolescent or individual. Or maybe your strongest memories are object inspired—your first apartment in the city, your first camera, or your first home. When beginning your project choose a starting point and watch where your memories flow.

The importance of memory

You might find yourself more inspired by stories you have heard and remembered. Think about why such stories have stayed with you and how your writing might better preserve them for generations to come. Chances are, if you've remembered something for this long then maybe there's a lesson learned, a questioned answered or begging to be asked. If you can recognize why certain memories are important to you, why these tales are burning to be told, then perhaps you can begin to identify some of your life's recurring themes. Whatever you remember has the potential to reveal something important about you; how you recall any event will always be different from how it's been preserved in the mind of your sister, husband, or best friend.

Revisiting old journals is an excellent way to exercise your writer's memory. Details recorded on the scene of an important experience or event, along with emotional reactions and thoughts, can help bring your current descriptions to life.

VOICES OF THE MASTERS

Václav Havel, a Czechoslovakian playwright who was
elected president of his country in 1989, was previously
imprisoned for his involvement with the Czech human
rights movement. This period of incarceration is the subject
of his memoir, *Disturbing the Peace*, which is presented
as a series of questions and answers, resulting from months
of conversations with Karel Hvízd'ala, a Czech journalist.
In the following extract, Havel explains the limitations
imposed upon his craft by the prison system and the way
they influenced his writing, and how being imprisoned
compelled him to review his own life and work out themes
in his head before committing them to paper:

> *We were allowed to write one four-page letter home a
> week. It had to be legible, with nothing corrected or
> crossed out, and there were strict rules
> about margins and graphic and stylistic
> devices (we were forbidden, for example, to
> use quotation marks, to underline words,
> use foreign expressions, etc.)....*
>
> *By the very nature of things in prison,
> you're forced to think a little more about
> yourself, about the meaning of your actions,
> about questions pertaining to your own
> Being. The letters gave me a chance to
> develop a new way of looking at myself and
> examining my attitudes to the fundamental
> things in life.... All week long I would
> develop my essays in my head—at work,
> during exercises, before going to bed—and
> then on Saturday, amid constant
> interruption, I would write them out in a
> kind of wild trance.*

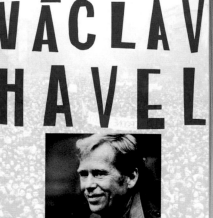

NATIONAL BESTSELLER

VÁCLAV HAVEL

"Scrupulous and sensitive... a gem of modest self-revelation
by a man skeptical about heroes who in fact became 'the
conscience of his nation.'" —*Los Angeles Times Book Review*

DISTURBING THE PEACE

*Václav Havel's involvement
with "Charter 77," a civil
rights manifesto, landed him
in prison for five years. It
was here that he spent hours
deeply examining his
motivation behind his beliefs
so he could one day express
it in his books.*

Why write?

One of the greatest benefits of writing your life story is self-discovery. But there are many other reasons to write—to share, to inspire, to warn, to justify, to celebrate, to entertain, or just to record. Perhaps you envisage a collection of personal essays or an album of photographs, collages, and poems; no matter the form that your project eventually takes, it will be personal to you and your own story.

Inventing the Truth, edited by William Zinsser, is a collection of essays that explores the memoir-writing experience of eight American writers. One of these writers, Russell Baker, a journalist, essayist, and humorist, states that he began writing his memoir long before he ever imagined it, when he started composing letters to his adolescent children: "I wanted my children to know that they were part of a long chain of humanity extending deep into the past and that they had some responsibility for extending it into the future."

VOICES OF THE MASTERS

Ian Frazier, another humorist and nonfiction writer, who also contributed to *Inventing the Truth,* found a collection of family papers dating back to 1855 after his parents died.

Using this as the catalyst for his book *Family,* he researched and wrote about his ancestors to give some meaning to their existence and to discover the larger forces of history that affected them. In *Inventing the Truth* Frazier writes:

From the start of writing Family *I needed to know that I had a plot. My plot was the disintegration of the Protestant establishment.... A parallel plot of the book is the attempt to give meaning to my parents' lives.... The two plots...coincide at the point of the death of my parents and the earlier death of my brother. A hundred years ago, before the Protestant enterprise hopped the rails, people would have known how to deal with those tragedies.... So it struck me that one of the meanings of my parents' lives was how they reacted to this disintegration of religious values....*

Old letters, photographs, objects, and journals, along with favorite places and songs, can help bring you back to the place in your past that you are aiming to explore.

VOICES OF THE MASTERS

V. S. Naipaul, a writer of fiction and nonfiction, was born in Trinidad and later emigrated to England when he won a scholarship to Oxford. In an essay entitled "The Writer and India" from his book *Reading and Writing—A Personal Account,* Naipaul writes about his relationship with the country of his forefathers. He chooses to explore the pain of his own position, looking deep into the soul of India and its past and present secrets, and to evaluate the experiences of life and reading that shaped his growth as a writer.

India was the greater hurt. It was a subject country. It was also the place from whose very great poverty our grandfathers had had to run away in the late nineteenth century. The two Indias were separate. The political India, of the freedom movement, had its great names. The other, more personal India was quite hidden; it vanished when memories faded. It wasn't an India we could read about. It wasn't Kipling's India, or E. M. Forster's, or Somerset Maugham's; and it was far from the somewhat stylish India of Nehru and Tagore….

It was to this personal India, and not the India of independence and its great names, that I went when the time came. I was full of nerves. But nothing had prepared me for the dereliction I saw. No other country I knew had so many layers of wretchedness, and few countries were as populous. I felt I was in a continent where, separate from the rest of the world, a mysterious calamity had occurred. Yet what was so overwhelming to me, so much in the foreground, was not to be found in the modern-day writing I knew, Indian or English. In one Kipling story an Indian famine was a background to an English romance; but generally in both English and Indian writing the extraordinary distress of India, when acknowledged, was like something given, eternal, something to be read only as background. And there were, as always, those who thought they could find a special spiritual quality in the special Indian distress.

V. S. Naipaul developed his skills and found his unique voice in the way all writers have to: by writing and continuing to write. To ensure the success of your life story project, make time to write—ideally every day—and adopt a writer's discipline from the start.

How to use this book

How to Write Your Life Story is divided into three sections: Generating Ideas, Organizing and Expressing Your Ideas, and Finishing Touches.

In Generating Ideas, you'll learn about the different approaches you can take to writing your story and what you should consider before you start. There are suggestions, examples, and writing exercises designed to help you generate memories and ideas and hone in on themes you might like to explore. By the end of this section you will have a collection of material that you can then begin to draw together into a structured whole, following the advice given in the second section.

Organizing and Expressing Your Ideas covers the various elements of the craft that make up memoir writing—such as character, dialogue, plot, and setting—to enable you to improve on your first drafts. You will also need to consider your readership in detail and determine how best to tie your story together: what structure or form your life story should take.

Finishing Touches will guide you as you assemble your final project and undertake the process of revision. You will discover how to combine text and images effectively and explore page design and digital display. You will also get advice on finding an agent and on different publishing possibilities.

Do not start generating ideas—the sooner, the better. *How to Write Your Life Story* will help inspire you to create a compelling and memorable account of your own life—a journey that begins the moment you commit your first idea to the page.

Generating ideas based on your own life experiences will help you structure your life story, which can then be honed and refined into a more polished form.

Part One
Generating Ideas

Choosing an Approach

Everyone has a life story, and it's up to you to decide how you want to tell yours—what approach to take. It's a personal journey, and you need to ask how deep within yourself you want to dig and what your purpose is. Are you looking to heal past wounds or forgive yourself for bad choices you have made, or do you simply wish to celebrate your family? Are you writing your story to recover some kind of loss, to discover what lies behind negative behavioral patterns that you can't help repeating, or were your travels so remarkable you feel they must be shared? Are you out to preserve your entire life story or are you simply plucking one piece of fruit from the family tree?

Who is your audience?

Whatever your reason for writing, you also need to decide on your intended audience before you get started. What kind of reader are you writing for? Your preferred audience will influence your final presentation, so you need to decide who your audience is (see pages 90–95 and 140–141 for a more detailed discussion of audience).

Private journey

Let's say you want to embark upon a path of self-discovery, a private journey that is strictly for your eyes only. If this is the path you choose, you may want to focus your attention less on the final presentation of your project and more on the journey itself. Like any other life story project, this one will begin with the challenge of excavating your past, and as a result you may find yourself reliving difficult experiences, making this a potentially upsetting (and possibly, cathartic) process. However, organizing these episodes in your life through your writing will help you better understand your experiences and how they helped form the individual you are today.

Your personal past might not be an easy place to revisit, but the journey will gain you understanding, perspective, remembrance of details, and depth—the tools you'll need to capture your life story on the page.

Family story

If you want to document and share your story with family or friends, then a scrapbook or journal (a polished version of this format, as opposed to a daily journal that you add to each day) might best suit your needs.

You may have a collection of photographs and ephemera that you want to piece together as a record of a vacation or to commemorate someone special. Perhaps you wish to serve as your children's memory, preserving for the future the lives they are too young to remember. If you are telling the story for your family and not for publication, you can use this book to help you collect the different threads of your story and assemble the pieces to make a satisfying account.

> Perhaps you wish to serve as your children's memory.

We'll explore ways to enlist all of your creative energies, using a variety of exercises, including poetry writing and drawing up a family tree, identifying life patterns, and how best to lay out all the ephemera you collected on a trip overseas.

Writing for publication

If your intention is to share your memoir with the world, it's a good idea to use the first part of this book to generate ideas and the second to organize and script them. Keep in mind, though, that preparing your story for the harsh scrutiny of the publishing industry and the reading public requires dedication and skill—but don't let this intimidate you. This book will guide you through the necessary steps, including advice on how to publish your work in literary magazines and how to research literary agents.

Great-Grandma, with Grandma on the left

Grandma on her 21st birthday

My family

Uncovering the secrets and lives of past generations—what held families together and tore individuals apart— can be your greatest contribution to those who come next.

Deciding on Your Story

Where to begin? Deciding on your story is usually easier than you think; often, it develops a life of its own and grows without much conscious intention on the writer's part. However, there are a few decisions you can make early on that will help determine how your story unfolds.

Alone or in collaboration?

First, consider whether the journey you are about to undertake will be a solo or collaborative effort (see also pages 142–143). You may change your mind as your enthusiasm grows. Once you have begun your journey, you may find you want a reader or two to help you edit and revise your work or just offer you some feedback; you may even find yourself in a writer's workshop, asking for additional help from other people who are in a similar position and have faced similar challenges.

> **It's always interesting to have more than one interpretation of a relationship.**

If your aim is to document your life in a relationship with someone, then you may want to invite him or her to join you—your significant other, your mother, your son, a friend. It's always interesting to have more than one interpretation of a relationship or an event, and sharing the work will make the task less daunting. You can share both the burdens and the pleasures of the experience.

Maybe you have a collection of correspondence between you and a friend that you jointly wish

to shape into a narrative. There are no limits to numbers in a collaboration. For example, if your family spent a month traveling around Mexico, you might want to include every single family member's story and personal mementos at some point in your travelogue.

Whether you choose to work solo or with someone else, it's important to have goals. They help you stay focused and motivated, even when you experience writer's block. Maybe your scrapbook is a gift for your partner and you want to finish it by your anniversary; or maybe your project will end once your children leave home. Deadlines, even minor ones, are motivators. Whatever the nature of your project, draw up a schedule and try your best to stick to it. The schedule will help you keep going until the project is complete.

Writing your life story with someone who shared it alongside you adds another chapter to your relationship.

Research style

The type of research you are willing to do will also determine what story you tell. Do you relish the idea of spending hours in the library, researching your family's history online, or poring over old periodicals and documents? If so, your story will evolve from the piles of information you collect, as it pertains to you. But if your project is intended more as a kind of personal therapy, your research will start from within.

> If your project is intended as a kind of personal therapy, your research will start from within.

Travel back in time by revisiting old postcards, papers, and magazines. Find out exactly what surrounded your life at the time; give your account some context.

Researching through memories, digging up dreams, and excavating your personal history to uncover what has been forgotten is a more introspective form of research, requiring unflinching self-reflection. That doesn't necessarily mean sitting in a chair and waiting for insight. You fell in love in Sofia 20 years ago? Now might be the time to revisit the Bulgarian capital. Walk the streets in search of memory triggers, taking notes on how things have changed in the place, within yourself, and at home.

The beauty of the writing process is that you don't need to have a clear idea of where you're headed to make a start. Approach your research with an open mind and a sense of adventure and you'll be surprised where it leads you. You may not have decided how many other people, if any, you want to share in your story, or how ambitious your project will be. The best way to find out is to begin gathering material, even if that means nothing more than sitting at a desk, searching your memory and writing some notes. Perhaps you don't yet know which aspects of your life you want to focus on. Continue working through this book, trying the suggested writing exercises, and you will soon find yourself inundated with ideas.

Internet access means you don't need to travel to the nearest library every time a new question comes up, like the name of a year's most popular tune or the date a certain event occurred. The answers are now never far from your desk.

Identifying Your Motivation

What first inspired you to write? Did you keep a journal as a safe place to divulge your secrets or as a refuge from an unhappy life? Did you start writing because the process enabled you to understand what was happening in your life or because you wanted to describe what you saw, to observe and document the world around you? Look at your collection of photographs and mementos. Do you keep this collection in order to remember where you've been and what you've done? Would you like to share it with family and friends but haven't because you don't want to overwhelm them with boxes full of unorganized bits and pieces? If you don't know how to present your life story, think about your motivations for writing. They will help you find a place to begin.

Finding a focus

It's often said that you should write about what you know. It's easier to communicate if you're familiar with and passionate about your subject matter, and you'll encounter fewer stumbling blocks. What are you drawn to in life? Is it your experience of being a parent? Then perhaps you want to explore or document your role—your relationships with your children, your observations of their development and growth, what being a parent was like for your mother and father, and how their roles might have influenced you.

Is travel your passion? Did you pore over *National Geographic* when you were a child? Do you have a collection of snapshots, tickets, and maps that you'd like to display? Did you research the history, local cultures, and customs of your destinations before leaving home, then document this information along with your travel experiences in notebooks? How did seeing something new change your life? You may want to use your wealth of information, experiences, and passion to construct your story as a travelogue.

Next time you travel, pack a journal and record all of the details you might someday forget—the name of your favorite dish, the white-walled village that blinded you with reflected sunlight, and the name of the fiesta that overtook the town for a day. You'll be glad of the references when you start to write.

Class of '57

EIGHT WEEK'S REPORT

This is your child's report; it shows his grade and progress of each eight week's work in religious training. Please examine it carefully. We are interested in your children, and it is our privilege to help you in your duty of teaching them to know, love and serve God. Without your cooperation we cannot succeed.

	Oct. Nov.	Dec. Jan.	Feb. Mar.	Apr. May	Year's Rating
ATTENDANCE					
Number of Sessions	9	8	8		
Present	8	8	8		
Absent	1	2	0		
RELIGIOUS INSTRUCTION					
Class Work	B	A	A		
Home Work	A⁻	A	A		
Conduct	B	B	A		
Effort	B	A	A		

Grades A (100 - 90) Excellent   B (89 - 80) Good
C (79 - 70) Fair   D (69 - 60) Failure

*My school report
first semester*

My first job, 1962

If your inspiration lies in another individual or in a specific place, then you could examine either in relation to yourself—the influence, the role, the point at which she or it inspired you to change—while expanding on the subject to include history, how the person or place changed, and the effect she or it had on others besides you. Maybe you're more interested in concentrating on a specific period in time: your school years, the Vietnam War or World War I or II, a divorce, the beginning of a new career, an illness. These subjects could be explored in a journal, a scrapbook, or a memoir.

Whether the subject is cooking, cars, clothing, movies, music, birds, or architecture, you can incorporate your passions so that they either become the focus of your story or a significant part of it. They might even suggest a structure for your project: a new chapter for every car you have owned or every bird you have seen, for example. If you like to collect recipes, you could choose to display them alongside stories of how they were obtained, including the actual occasions for which the recipes were prepared, with photographs of each celebration or each dish.

Rummage through those shoe boxes and pull out and preserve forgotten documents. Tie your school years together, and promise to take notes on whatever happens next—a new job or career, a big purchase, a trip, or a new relationship.

Memory Triggers

A memory trigger is anything that helps bring your past to the surface. It could be a piece of music, an old photograph, your diary, an object, or a letter. These triggers are also launchpads from which you can begin to construct your story. Lists, in particular, serve as strong memory triggers, and list-making is a great way to generate a wealth of ideas. Experiencing writer's block? Make a list. Lists can be made of anything; they can even become a poem. Let your lists show how you have become the individual you are today and use them to start writing.

List building

Once you have tried some of the lists suggested in the box, many more lists will suggest themselves to you. Make as many lists as you feel you need, then with a list in hand consider the story that surrounds each listed item. You might script a rough outline of one particular event or simply start writing. The more time you spend on your writing, the more details you will recall.

For instance, your story may involve many places (see pages 30–31 for a detailed discussion of setting). Perhaps you moved a lot as a child or traveled extensively as an adult. List the places where you learned and/or changed the most. Compare and contrast the different settings. Did you fit in? Think about yourself in relation to the settings. Were you in conflict with the environment or at ease? How did your environment inspire you to act? What effect did all of this motion have on you? Did moving around as a child make you a restless adult, or did being on the road enable you to feel free?

You can use other memory triggers to build upon this initial stage—photographs of people or events, music from that era, or your journals from

that time. Once you start remembering, you won't be able to stop. Keep in mind that ideas and recollections may come to you at any point during the night or day. Jot down your memories to use in your story; don't let them get away from you.

Moving from the city to the country can evoke a host of emotions. Make a list of the changes you faced to examine if this event may have shaped you into the adult you are today.

WRITER'S WORKSHOP

Lists are an excellent source for generating ideas. Below are a few topics worth exploring.

- Best friends who have passed through your life. Say how these relationships began and ended.

- Turning points—the decisions that changed your life.

- Times when your emotions felt out of control.

- People who have influenced, disappointed, inspired, abandoned, supported, hurt, accepted, rejected, pleased, or informed you.

- Goals that you have strived hard to achieve.

- Regrets.

- Secrets you have kept.

- People you have loved and the ways in which they returned your love.

- Your favorite words.

- Moments when you were afraid.

- Your favorite foods, movies, songs, books, restaurants, walks, drives, characters, or bars, and the memories you associate with each.

- What you could never live without. What do these people/things/activities mean to you?

- Your happiest moments.

- Childhood events that stand tall in your memory.

Make a list of all the many and varied people who have passed through your life. Some will have been very important, others will have been peripheral to your life experience, but all will have had some impact on your unique life story.

- Encounters with strangers, including those with whom you later developed relationships.

- What you still hope to achieve and why these goals are important to you.

- World events that have had a powerful impact on your life.

- Places to which you have traveled, noting which were your favorites and the ones you disliked. Note which places you have revisited and the ways in which they had changed.

- Character traits that have clearly been adopted from your mother, father, older brother, or aunt. Which of these do you cherish and which do you hope to leave behind?

- Things you wish you could change about the world, your past, or yourself.

- A lists of firsts—your first kiss, first hurt, the first time you realized your life was your own, your first fight, first love, first big decision, or crush.

- Recurring dreams.

- Your most private fantasies.

- The incidents or moments behind your most cherished photographs.

Soul Searching

Dragging up the submerged memories of your life is not always easy. Seeking the truth often hurts and may be something that you are loath to face. Unfortunately, there is no easy way to get around the pain, but it may be precisely what brings your story to life. The more you feel, the closer you get to the experience; the closer you get to the experience, the more alive it becomes on the page. What better way to access the details of your past than to make yourself relive it?

Stepping back

Reliving fond memories is pleasurable, but it's life's struggles that tend to make for more interesting reading. Looking at yourself through a microscope requires objectivity and work. To avoid making judgments on the page, which makes characters two-dimensional and loses the reader's trust (see pages 124–125), the writer has to forgive. The mother who left, the brother who lied, the best friend who betrayed—no matter how awful the crime, no one wants to read the words of a vituperative writer (and if you are writing for your eyes only, one-sided subjectivity is not a healthy path to recovery).

> Let go of the negative feelings that have prevented you from moving on.

In order to examine a situation objectively, you must step back. What does this mean exactly? You must examine your behavior, accept responsibility for wrongdoing, and let go of the negative feelings that have prevented you from moving on. Sometimes it's tough to do it alone, in which case seeking guidance doesn't hurt. The support of a family member or friend, a counselor, or therapist can help get you through the most difficult times.

It's easier to maintain balance when you stand back and assess the situation. Who came to your aid and strengthened your stance when you most needed it?

VOICES OF THE MASTERS

Kathryn Harrison's novel, *Thicker Than Water,* is a story about a young woman's incestuous relationship with her father. She later rewrote it as a memoir entitled *The Kiss.* If you find it hard to distance yourself from a remembered situation, you might try writing your story in the third person—put someone else through your life story—before rewriting it in the first person. In an interview with *Bookforum,* the interviewer broaches how Harrison did this in her writing:

Bookforum: *A. L. Kennedy, in a recent interview in these pages, said that while writing fiction she could be more emotionally revealing than when writing memoir. You've written four memoirs, and your first novel,* Thicker Than Water, *is very close to the story in your first memoir,* The Kiss. *I recently reread* Thicker Than Water *and found it more intense and disturbing than the memoir.*

K.H.: *…one of the motivations for writing* The Kiss *was that I had fictionalized the story. Because* Thicker Than Water *was a typically autobiographical first novel, with aspects changed around and disguised, I felt disappointed in it and in myself: I knew that there was a story that was real and one that needed to be owned. To novelize a story of incest is to participate in the societal imperative to always lie about it, to say it's not happening, or that you made it up. For that reason, I wanted to disown that novel as soon as it was published.* The Kiss *is intentionally stripped-down because I wanted to reveal that archetypal triangle of the parents and the child. The shell-shocked, present-tense narration reveals some of the experience of being in a relationship like that, in which you are in a kind of cottony, emotionally vacant state—it's the only way to get through things like that. In a sense, the books are separate truths that, in the end, complement each other.*

While you may not be exploring the same subject matter as Harrison, the emotional reality behind your story may have the same intensity. So try writing fiction first; it may help you to access, accept, and publish the truth later on.

Time Lines

Another way to jump-start your memory is to construct a time line. Not only will this exercise help you organize your story and thereby lend it structure, but it will also help illuminate the dark spaces between your memories. It is an excellent way of planning your story, since it helps to draw together the many threads of your life.

Finding your starting point

Think about when your story begins. Is it the day you were born, the day you got married, the day you found out a loved one was terminally ill, the moment your daughter was born? What experience was the catalyst for change? Was it a decision you made or an incident that was beyond your control? Whatever it was, begin your time line here. Think about the people involved, the setting (did it change?), and what happened next. Break your line down into as many specifics as possible. Allow branches to grow above and below each situation and/or experience that falls on your line. Add more branches as your story develops.

Adding detail

Once your time line is complete, you can start employing possible story outlines (see also pages 128–131) or lists. For each branch of your time line, outline the experience as it occurred, chronologically, or simply brainstorm and free-associate while keeping notes. What was the result of your decision or actions? What were your feelings at the time? Was any other situation affected by this one? Looking back, how have your views changed? Would you have done things differently? Do you have any regrets? Use your lists to gather details, which will help illuminate your memories and bring them to life.

Themes

What falls on and off your time lines will not only help determine the nature of your story, but will also help identify its themes—the messages of your story that link all its parts together (see also pages 34–35 and 122–123). The time line given on the following page is dominated by the writer's relationships and travels; the theme that runs through it is her restless search to find and define herself through experience, suggesting that this is a late bloomer's coming-of-age story.

> With your time line and lists at hand, look for similarities in your situations or decisions.

With your time line and your lists at hand, look for similarities in your situations or decisions. Are there recurring feelings that thread through your time line? Are these feelings a result of your actions? Are the actions repetitive in any way? Is there a pattern of behavior to be found in your relationships, your career, your moods, or in your interactions with others?

Keep your data organized. You might want to keep your notes together in a notebook so that you can access them easily when you begin to write. This will make the whole process easier.

WRITER'S WORKSHOP

Create a sample time line to organize your thoughts.

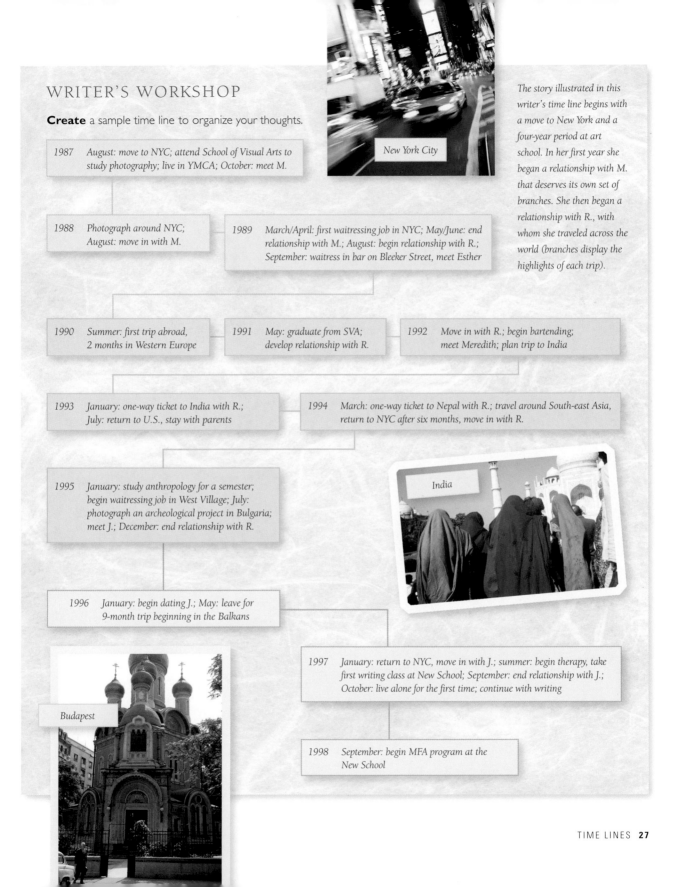

New York City

The story illustrated in this writer's time line begins with a move to New York and a four-year period at art school. In her first year she began a relationship with M. that deserves its own set of branches. She then began a relationship with R., with whom she traveled across the world (branches display the highlights of each trip).

1987 *August: move to NYC; attend School of Visual Arts to study photography; live in YMCA; October: meet M.*

1988 *Photograph around NYC; August: move in with M.*

1989 *March/April: first waitressing job in NYC; May/June: end relationship with M.; August: begin relationship with R.; September: waitress in bar on Bleeker Street, meet Esther*

1990 *Summer: first trip abroad, 2 months in Western Europe*

1991 *May: graduate from SVA; develop relationship with R.*

1992 *Move in with R.; begin bartending; meet Meredith; plan trip to India*

1993 *January: one-way ticket to India with R.; July: return to U.S., stay with parents*

1994 *March: one-way ticket to Nepal with R.; travel around South-east Asia, return to NYC after six months, move in with R.*

India

1995 *January: study anthropology for a semester; begin waitressing job in West Village; July: photograph an archeological project in Bulgaria; meet J.; December: end relationship with R.*

1996 *January: begin dating J.; May: leave for 9-month trip beginning in the Balkans*

1997 *January: return to NYC, move in with J.; summer: begin therapy, take first writing class at New School; September: end relationship with J.; October: live alone for the first time; continue with writing*

Budapest

1998 *September: begin MFA program at the New School*

Character

Before you begin to incorporate the cast of characters from your time line into your life story, you need to gather as much information about these individuals as you can. Once you have all the data at hand, you can decide what's relevant to your story, what details are worth developing, and what to exclude.

Exploring your characters

From your time line you should have a picture of where and under what circumstances people appeared in your life. You can now make an outline for each character: Create a list of relationship phases and significant events. You could use a separate index card for every incident or encounter, which may aid the development of your structure later on. Consider what approach will best enable you to dissect your characters on the page. Do you want to explore individuals based on their character traits, their accomplishments, or their effects and/or influences on you, or do you simply want to explore your relationships chronologically? Don't worry at this stage about exactly which people you want to include or how much you want to focus on one individual, because right now you're still just collecting information.

VOICES OF THE MASTERS

Jamaica Kincaid's memoir *My Brother* revolves around her relationship with her youngest sibling and his battle with AIDS. As Kincaid explores this complicated relationship, she takes the reader with her on a journey of self-exploration and discovery. If you already know that the life story you are constructing will explore a specific relationship, then you'll need to focus just as much on the relationship as on the individual (see also pages 32–33).

> *At the end of one day, when he was in the hospital and I had been sitting with him for most of the time, watching his body adjust to the AZT medicine I had brought to him because I had been told that it was not available in Antigua, I said to him that nothing good could ever come of his being ill, but all the same I wanted to thank him for making me realize that I loved him, and he asked if I meant that ("But fo' true?") and I said yes, I did mean that.*

You can ensure the characters in your story come across as three-dimensional by building a detailed profile of each. Ask yourself what they enjoy. What foods do they like to eat? What makes them laugh?

Collecting character data

No matter how well you think you know someone, you need to collect data and withhold judgments before writing in order to make each individual come to life on the page.

> You won't want to include everything about the person, only what's relevant to the story.

How can you make your characters seem as individual as they are in life? Start by asking yourself what makes these people so different from everyone else. How did she dress? Were her gestures unusual? How did he fill a room with his presence and physically interact with others? Was her face particularly expressive? Did he always use certain phrases? Did he have a tragic flaw, such as trouble perceiving reality, a history of making bad choices, or selective memory? How did she react in a moment of crisis?

To consider this person wholly, make a list of his or her best qualities, favorite foods, words, music, clothes, loves and hates, fears, habits, secrets, outlook on life, faults, and expectations. When it comes to writing, you won't want to include everything about the person, only what's relevant to the story. Nevertheless, it's useful to have this information at hand because it helps bring the person to life in your mind.

Consider, too, the role that these people have played in your life. Who served as your antagonist and how did he oppose or obstruct your goals? Consider her contradictions: What effect did these inner conflicts have on others? Was he a man who hated having his wife noticed, but who loved to objectify women? Just as you need to look deep within yourself, you also need to reflect upon your characters and allow them room to breathe.

Portraying individuality

You can ensure the characters in your story come across as three-dimensional by building a detailed profile of each before you start. Ask yourself what they enjoy. What foods do they like to eat? Where do they feel most at home? What makes them laugh? What is important to them?

Remember to use words or expressions that the individual would use, or see if you can describe their voice or the sound of their laughter.

You need to show your reader exactly why you loved and cherished a certain individual—what you shared, what he brought out in you, why you wanted to break it off.

Setting

What places fall on your time line and had a significant impact on your life—the house where you grew up, your elementary school, or the front seat of the Chevy where you first kissed the girl who later became your wife? Just as with characters, you need to collect information about your setting before deciding what to include.

Place as a character

If your life story involves a specific place—Toronto in the 1970s, a hotel in Italy, the safe-haven where you focused on recovery—you should allow the setting to become a character. Construct it in such a way that it becomes a presence that influences and affects the other characters in your story.

VOICES OF THE MASTERS

Anatole Broyard, in his memoir, *Kafka Was the Rage*, makes Greenwich Village a central figure in a story that charts his development as a young man.

The setting of this story is not only the place—Greenwich Village—but also the period; each aspect has a significant impact on the characters in the book, and most especially on the author.

The Village was as close in 1946 as it would ever come to Paris in the twenties…. The streets and bars were full of writers and painters and the kind of young men and women who liked to be around them. In Washington Square would-be novelists and poets tossed a football near the fountain and girls just out of Ivy League colleges looked at the landscape with art history in their eyes….

It was a loneliness that walked the streets of the Village and filled the bars, loneliness that made it seem such a lively place.

Looking back at the late 1940s, it seems to me now that Americans were confronting their loneliness for the first time. Loneliness was like the morning after the war, a great hangover.

Your story may be set in a neighborhood, or it could be a travelogue that takes place all over the world, or perhaps it is set in a meaningful place that is not your home— where you spent your holidays, for example.

The bigger picture

The same technique applies to researching setting as to researching character. If your story is situated in one place, think about the relevance of time and history on this place. What did it look like, sound like, smell like, feel like? What was the texture of the landscape—sharp, hard and angular, arid and scrubby, or soft and chalky? How was this space inhabited and by whom? Did it ever change? What was your relationship to this place and what do you associate with it?

Consider too the wider context: how your place and time relate to history and to the world. Is it a peaceful time or one of turmoil? What effect did the culture and/or current events have on society and on you? Just as you want your characters to step off the page, you also want your reader to be able to envision your setting and to inhabit it as if it were her own.

> **Consider how your place and time relate to history and to the world.**

VOICES OF THE MASTERS

Virginia Woolf muses on London in winter in her personal essay "Street Haunting—A London Adventure," written in 1930, in which she is describing "the greatest pleasure of town life in winter"—readily exchanging the solitude of her work for a ramble through the streets of the capital.

How beautiful a London street is then, with its islands of light, and its long groves of darkness, and on one side of it perhaps some tree-sprinkled, grass-grown space where night is folding herself to sleep naturally, and as one passes the iron railing, one hears those little cracklings and stirrings of leaf and twig which seem to suppose the silence of fields all round them, an owl hooting, and far away the rattle of a train in the valley. But this is London, we are reminded; high among the bare trees are hung oblong frames of reddish yellow light—windows; there are points of brilliance burning steadily like low stars—lamps; this empty ground, which holds the country in it and its peace is only a London square, set about by offices and houses where at this hour fierce lights burn over maps, over documents, over desks where clerks sit….

Woolf's city, like the country, is full of soft sights and sounds, blanketed by winter's early darkness. The people are somewhere behind glowing windows that illuminate the outdoors like stars. Her long sentences help slow the reader's pace; we stroll through the winter by her side.

Relationships

Intimate relationships—whether with a lover, a child, a mentor, or a friend—can bring out a variety of emotions and behavior that, had you remained alone, would not have existed. How have these relationships changed your life? If the focus of your story is your relationship with another person, the beginning of your time line may mark the occasion on which you came together, and the remainder of the time line may chart the shared experience that ensued.

Analyzing the relationship

Having already taken a close look at the characters that have appeared in your life, it's now time to examine who and what you were together. Think of the person you were when you met. What was your life like, how did you want or expect it to change, and what did you feel? How did you meet and what was your initial reaction to the encounter—were you overwhelmed when you first held your newborn, or swept away by your first encounter with your future best friend?

Make a list of the qualities that this particular person brought out in you: jealousy, kindness, determination, or compassion. Was your relationship balanced? Did one person contribute more, work harder, or live faster, or were you evenly paced? These questions can help identify how the relationship changed your life.

Relationships are living organisms that constantly evolve and need nourishment; some require more maintenance than others to survive. What did you get out of the relationship compared to what you put in? How did your relationship change you—in terms of your needs, interactions, expectations, and trust? Did your relationship with this individual coincide with anything else in your life, such as a tragic loss, a major change, an accomplished goal, or a new outlook on life? Metaphorically, how would you describe your chosen relationship—an olive tree, a sunrise, a train wreck? Metaphors are an effective way of describing something without having to get involved in too many distracting and often unnecessary details. They can also help to open up your imagination, triggering thoughts and ideas that would not have occurred to you otherwise.

In order to chart your connections, create another series of lists, and use these guidelines to compare relationships in order to identify patterns or themes. These patterns may help you determine the subject of your writing.

When writing about a relationship, imagine what your life would be like if you had never met this person. Then you'll have an idea of how much he or she has affected you and how much you've changed.

Our first dance

Our wedding day

25 happy years

Learning from a relationship

If the relationship you're exploring is still ongoing, consider how it makes you feel on a daily basis. What are your expectations for the future? How do you nurture the other person to ensure these goals will be attained?

Or is your relationship long over? If so, chart it through to the end. If something other than relocation or death terminated it, reflect on how and why this happened. How did you feel when it was over? Did you both agree to separate or did it happen against your will? Looking back, was there anything different you would have done? How long was your healing process and what did you miss most when the person was gone? What did you learn from the experience and could you apply that lesson later on in life? How different does the experience seem now from when you were involved? Use the answers as indicators of how you have changed and to help you identify additional patterns of behavior.

Knowing the significance of your relationships will help you decide how much emphasis they deserve. Charting personal growth and change will help you determine how to structure your story. By dissecting your past, you're creating pieces of a puzzle that you are now free to reassemble. With the experience long behind you, you may find the pieces coming together to create a picture of your life story that surprises you and that you hadn't expected.

Consider what fed your relationships to keep them strong, and what they required to grow—did you find comfort in stability, habit, and ritual, or in challenge and change?

> Charting personal growth and change will help you determine how to structure your story.

Patterns and Themes

By now you should have a healthy collection of time lines, lists, and outlines—the facts that will form the backbone of your work. The next step is to draw together your data and analyze it by looking for patterns—in emotions, relationships, behavior, and choices—and themes (see also pages 122–123).

Identifying your life themes

A smart man once said that everyone has three life themes that he or she addresses repeatedly. Though you may not recognize them until your project (or even your second or third work) is complete, it's important to narrow them down. First, consider your emotions. What themes are you drawn to in books, music, and movies—social isolation, the hopefulness of romance, the desire to overcome weaknesses or obstacles? Are there certain emotions you find yourself reliving, no matter the time or place—euphoria, loneliness, a need for love or control? What roles have you tended to assume in group situations or moments of crisis—the focused ringleader, the introspective individual, the outspoken clown? These questions may help identify your three life themes.

Second, referring to your paperwork from your previous work on relationships, look for repeating patterns—the circumstance of your meeting, your emotions, your strengths, your struggles, your ways of dealing with conflicts, what you've had to offer, and how each of your relationships came to an end. Think about the individuals to whom you became attached. Do they share any qualities—warm and loving, manipulative and withholding, adventurous, needy, strong? Why are you drawn to those who have passed through or remained in your life? What

Consider your contributions to group dynamics. Do you tend to lead or blend with the shadows? Are you optimistic when others encounter obstacles?

kinds of roles have you repeatedly played—the supportive parental figure, the roaming free agent, or the withdrawn recluse?

Third, reflect on your choices. Have they always been wise? Do you have many regrets? If so, are they the result of similar actions? Are you generally impulsive, or slow and thoughtful regarding your decisions? How have these behavioral traits worked for you? Have you learned from your mistakes, or have you made the same mistakes repeatedly? Do you always follow through on your thoughts and promises or have you often disappointed yourself and others? Look at how you go about attaining your goals and the results your actions achieve. Do you procrastinate or are

> Look at how you go about attaining your goals.

WRITER'S WORKSHOP

Analyzing patterns You can usually find patterns in any aspect of life that you wish to explore.

• *Your career:* How have you gone about setting and achieving your goals? How have you related to those who crossed your path? What has been your relationship to the work you have done?

• *Your travels:* What drew you to the places you have visited? How did you interact with local people and fellow travelers? What did you learn from your experiences?

• *Your faith:* How was it developed? When do you find yourself needing it most? How does it affect your relationships with others?

If you are writing about other people, you can examine their characters by asking the same questions.

Your high-school yearbooks will take you back to these formative years. Pick out friends in the photographs. What attracted you to them? How did the relationships play out over time?

you the one to overachieve? How has your behavior left you feeling emotionally? If you find yourself providing similar answers for a variety of situations or relationships, then chances are your interactions are being steered by your patterns in behavior.

> Perhaps your story revolves around a life-changing experience.

Cause and effect

Perhaps your story revolves around a life-changing experience. If so, you should examine how you changed. What effect did this experience have on you? Did it alter your beliefs or behavior? How did it affect those around you? Did your relationships change, and if so, why? Did this experience bring out aspects of your personality that you never knew existed, or did it build upon and exaggerate what was already there? With each answer you should be gaining further knowledge of yourself.

When you closely examine aspects of your life, you need to make note of cause and effect. As we shall see later on, the pattern of cause and effect is what constructs plot (see pages 108–109); being aware of the various subplots in your life will help direct your story as it unfolds.

Many of the perceptions you have of yourself are rooted in your experience of high school. What kind of character were you in class? Have you continued to play the same role?

Research

Have you ever considered researching your family history? Now that you're writing your life story, it might be a good time to start. Begin by making a family tree from your own knowledge. In the top tier, place yourself, your partner and children, and your brothers and sisters (if you have any); then in the tier below, add your parents and aunts and uncles; in a third tier, place your grandparents and their siblings, and so on. Go as far back in time as you can. Your stopping point indicates where your research needs to begin. If you have a partner willing to assist you, be ready to employ him or her; the journey ahead could be long, and you may find it more fun and less daunting to have a companion.

Interview family members

Courthouses, public libraries, public records offices, and places of worship are likely sources of information, but you should first find out what you can by checking with family members. Make a list of questions that will keep you focused on obtaining the information you need and tape record interviews if you can, to allow you to refer back to them and reflect upon what you have been told. Be sure to ask where family members lived, what institutions and societies (academic, religious, professional, political, sporting, artistic) they belonged to, where they worked, and where they are buried. This gives you a map of where you need to go when your live sources run dry, or to confirm or expand on what you've been told. Remember, people's memories can be faulty—fact check when you can. Ask if anyone has letters, diaries, photographs, or other memorabilia they are willing to share.

Decide at some point how deep you want your research to go. Are you looking simply to map out your family tree, or are you seeking to better understand the lives of every family member before you? Perhaps you're looking for something in between. You may decide at an early stage that

your interest is in tracing the maternal or paternal line only, for example.

Keep organized

From the beginning, document your sources systematically. Otherwise, you may find you have to start from scratch, should you decide to dig deeper. This will also enable other people to go straight to the source if need be. Keep a record of where you conducted your research, even if nothing valuable was found, to ensure you don't retrace your steps. Be sure to organize your material logically from the start—for example, designate a separate file for each person and color code each generation—so that you can easily find your material when you need it. Researching your family history might encourage questions you never knew to ask, not just about your predecessors but also about yourself. Try to keep an open mind and be ready to accept the answers that you find.

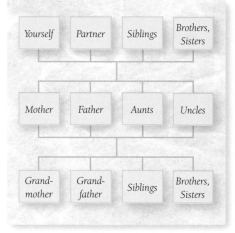

You can follow the simple scheme above when creating your own family tree.

Researching the records At town halls and courthouses you can find primary sources, such as birth and death certificates, marriage records, wills, and estate tax records. Local libraries usually have old city directories and newspapers that you can check for information on family members from the area regarding marriages, births, deaths, and other local news and gossip. Consult a specialist publication, such as Bev Kirschner Braun's *Crafting Your Own Heritage Album,* for detailed advice on how to do archival research, including consulting state land records, state pension records, census records, Native American records, vehicle registration and drivers' licenses, voter registrations, and poll tax records. Try the Internet for further information.

- On the federal level, the National Archives and Records Administration (NARA) (www.archives.gov) has information regarding census records, military records, pension files, passenger ship lists, and land records.

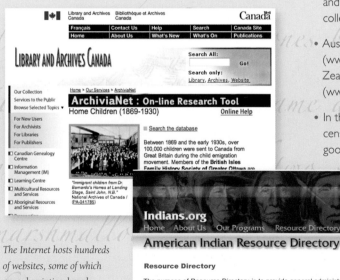

The Internet hosts hundreds of websites, some of which are subscription-based, although many are free. In the final pages of this book, you'll find a list of additional sites to explore.

- One of the largest free genealogy databases, Ancestor Hunt (www.ancestorhunt.com), is run by the Mormons and offers ways to search for family members, plus extensive links.

- African-Americans may want to contact the Afro-American Historical and Genealogical Society, Inc. (www.aahgs.org/).

- Native Americans might try the American Indian Resource Directory (www.indians.org/Resource/resource.html).

- Cyndi's List of Genealogy Sites (www.cyndislist.com) contains links to a host of useful sites covering adoption, immigration and naturalization, military resources worldwide, and much more.

- Genealogylinks.net (www.genealogylinks.net) is a helpful international site.

- Canadians wishing to research their roots can visit Genealogy Helplist Canada (www.rootsweb.com) and the Canadian Genealogy Centre (www.collectionscanada.ca/genealogy).

- Australians may want to try Genealogy Search Australia (www.searchwhateveraustralia.com.au); and New Zealanders can visit New Zealand Genealogy Links (www.genealogylinks.net/newzealand/).

- In the UK, the register of births, marriages, deaths, and censuses on the Internet (www.ukbmd.org.uk) is a good place to start.

Your Family's Origins

Whether or not you plan to reconstruct your family tree, you need to consider the places from which your family came. Your family origins inform not only your own history but also your tastes and culture. Knowledge of the ways and traditions of earlier generations will help to illuminate your own behavior traits and give you a better understanding of your family's place in society.

Looking at your origins

Perhaps your grandparents or great-grandparents came to America through Ellis Island. Consider what their lives were like. Were they a part of mass immigration, settling into a community with others from home, or did they seek to erase all traces of their past so that they might begin anew? If they did come via Ellis Island, you're fortunate, because many records exist and can be accessed online (www.ellisisland.org). A trip to the Ellis Island Immigration museum can also tell you what their journey might have been like, what possessions they might have carried with them, and what they might have encountered when they arrived. Or perhaps your ancestors immigrated to Canada, Australia, or New Zealand, in which case you could research their port of entry and the life they found on arriving there.

Traveling to the place from which your family came may be part of your project. This can be a journey into the unknown. You may not find what you expect—you may not even know what to expect. The journey may answer your questions—or it may create even more. Whatever the outcome, this journey, and not just the information you find, could form an interesting chapter in your life story, as well as adding to your understanding of your past.

Use all the resources available. If your family were immigrants, you could check out museum records, such as those at the Ellis Island Immigration museum.

Making connections

Use this knowledge about yourself when you begin writing your life story. Today different reasons encourage movement—career enhancement, ease of travel, regional preference, study opportunities, and relationships. This movement, if it's a tangible part of your past, is part of your story. You can recount your expectations before you moved, what the journey was like, and how your destination compared to what you imagined it would be. Describe the transition—making new friends, the language and new customs, learning your way around, or any sense of isolation or dislocation that the move may have led to. Consider what you missed once you got to your new location and whether these feelings surprised you. Perhaps you made the trip with others; think how their experience compared to yours. What is your relationship now to the place from which you came? Has it changed since you moved? This relocation might come to exemplify other highs or struggles in your life.

Modern travel has made it much easier for individuals and families to uproot and disconnect from their origins. How has relocation affected your own or your family's relationship to the land, culture, and habits left behind?

> Describe the transition—making new friends, learning your way around.

Not all peoples of the world have been fortunate enough to control their own destiny. Some have been expelled from their homelands and forced to relocate; others were captured and carried away as property. Though it may be painful to consider your ancestors having lived these lives, the knowledge will both empower you and honor their plight. If this is your history, what effect has it had on your ancestors, your people, and, more specifically, on your own life? You may be a member of a tight community as a result of such collective struggles, or perhaps you feel disenfranchised, continuing to confront the opposition that your ancestors faced.

Culture

While the culture of an age is generally specific to that time period, the culture of a particular social or ethnic group is usually transmitted from one generation to the next. Knowing about your family's origins allows you to pose and answer questions about your own culture. Consider what aspects of it have been passed from one generation to the next.

Many individuals who volunteer for the armed forces are following a family tradition. How have the decisions made by your forefathers influenced the choices you make today?

The role of religion

If religion is a part of your life, note whether it is something that's been practiced in your family for generations. The rituals, mores, and diet imposed by your faith may have played a large part in defining both who you are and the choices you

have made: the holidays you celebrate, the music you cherish, and the foods you prepare. Ask yourself how the role of religion has changed in your family over the years. While religion may not be the focus of your story, it might provide a powerful backdrop.

> While religion may not be the focus of your story, it might provide a backdrop.

Family culture

Often our tastes run so deep it seems they might be genetic—even our food preferences. Considering yourself from a cultural point of view, ask how your beliefs relate to the tenets of those who came before you—not just in how they pertain to religion or food, but also in how they pertain to politics, education, class, the arts, or athletics. Are you one in a long line? Has your family served in the military for as long as you can recall? Do you share a history of talented musicians? Do you come from a long line of conservatives?

Consider your rituals and habits, including the mundane ones—how you prepare your coffee, get ready for bed, spend your Sunday mornings, use your utensils, or decorate your home. You may find that you can recognize the influence of others in these everyday aspects of your life.

Other influences

It's important to look at your role within society to consider the impact of culture on your life and how it helped form the individual you are today. Think about what role culture plays outside of your family influences. Are you or have you been a member of any social clubs, athletic teams, or volunteer groups, or participated in subcultures based on music, religion, or hobbies? Perhaps you have bonded with others through significant past experiences such as fighting in a war, a tragedy, or your career. Ask yourself how these communities have helped shape you, what they were like in terms of the interactions, the rules, the individuals, the politics, the membership requirements, the competition, and the support, and what you gained from them.

Maybe you have been affiliated with social or political movements—antiwar protests, civil rights marches, or the women's movement. Think about what it was like to be a part of something much larger than yourself and what the social climate was at the time—one of peace, rebellion, reflection, or upheaval. Have you ever been affiliated with or loyal to a specific cause? Think about why you joined and whether you were able to contribute, or receive, what you had hoped. Maybe your mother's struggle with breast cancer led you to join support groups and attend fund-raising events, or your passion for improving local schools led you to assume an active role in your PTA or school community. Culture and community can help provide the setting for your life story, and place it in context.

Losing a loved one often motivates people to get involved, participate in fund-raisers. Such an experience could produce an inspirational story.

Anti-war rallies often provide hope for those whose cries fall on politicians' deaf ears. Perhaps the coming together with others who share your desire for more peaceful measures can be a topic on which you can expand.

Family Gatherings and Holidays

Search your memory and bring to mind your family gathered for a holiday or special occasion, whether it's Christmas, New Year, or your grandmother's birthday. Try to determine what stands out most about this event. Maybe a particular relative comes to mind, one who has influenced or changed your life. Or, at another level, perhaps you find yourself experiencing a strong emotion in response to this event—whether it's discomfort, fear, or hope. Are you drawn to the family changes that have occurred over the years—the marriages and separations, the newborns, and those who have fled the flock?

The treasure chest of a family gathering

Start generating a list of the elements that come to mind about a gathering that's significant for you— the family members, the food, the individual events that made this gathering memorable. Next, explore each element in depth. If it's the food, list the dishes special to your family. You may remember dishes that have been passed down over generations and specialty foods particular to your nationality. Maybe you want to include the recipes in your scrapbook or memoir. Was your grandmother's traditional cooking replaced by something better or worse once she passed away? Remember to employ all five of your senses. What did the gathering smell like? The dominant smell might be fresh bread, the roast in the oven, your aunt's perfume, or your uncle's cigar. What was the setting? Perhaps your grandfather's plush study, a restaurant, or your mother's formal dining room with its stiff chairs. How did you feel? Did you look forward to this gathering or did you dread it? Use these questions to explore your memory, and you'll find the answers will help you generate writing material.

Family gatherings, infrequent or not, are a bit like experiments in a lab: the chemistry between members, the life-saving formulas, the repetition and rituals, and the occasional blow-ups.

Consider your role as a child and then as an adult. How might it have changed? As a child did you act up and welcome attention? As an adult do you hold the family together or withhold until the gathering is over?

Your place in the family

The family is a mine of information and potential insights, whether it's your immediate family, your extended family, or the family you chose to create. It's your foundation, where you learned your patterns of behavior and social habits, where you were taught your sense of self-worth. Even if you're not planning to write about your family members, they're worth exploring not only for the way in which they may have influenced the choices you have made, but also as a point of comparison.

> **Are you most intrigued by your family and its history as a whole?**

Did your best friend's house full of siblings make your quiet life with Mom seem inadequate? Did experiencing your brother's difficult behavior teach you how not to behave? Has your close relationship with your sister led you to have specific expectations for all of your relationships? By examining your initial relationships, you'll gain a better understanding of the relationships you later developed.

Once you've addressed this topic, take note of what interests you most. Is it your own personal journey or struggle within your family? Are you most intrigued by your family and its history as a whole? Or is there one event, one individual, one road traveled that has had a significant impact on your life? Once you narrow your focus, you'll be able to revive the specific memories that will help reveal this particular aspect of your life.

Explore what distinguishes you from other families. Did you gather for unusual reasons? What is it about these get-togethers that you'd like to pass on?

Personal Interviews

The questions you will ask in an interview largely depend upon your motive. Is there a specific incident you want to learn more about, or are you trying to gain a general understanding of the person you are interviewing? Are you hoping to learn about a time period before you were born? Whatever your reason for interviewing someone, outline your questions beforehand so that you keep your focus and get the information you need. If possible, record or videotape your interviews so that you don't miss anything said.

Conducting the interview

Once you have decided on your topic, it's time to generate a list of questions. Keep in mind the personality of the individual you are interviewing and your relationship; make sure you are sensitive to the person's thoughts, beliefs, and experiences. If you are interviewing someone you don't know well and are trying to get a sense of how he can fill in the gaps of your past, ask questions that elicit basic facts, such as birth date and place, names of family members, education, employment, places where he lived, hobbies and passions, and so on.

If your aim is to learn about your ancestors, then you'll want to keep the questions focused on the past. For example, when interviewing your grandmother, ask her the names of her parents, grandparents, siblings, in-laws, nieces, and nephews. Where were these people born, where did they move, what did they do for a living, what levels of education did they achieve, when did they die, and where are they buried? If you have the time, you might ask her to recall stories that will bring these people to life or stories of the family's successes and tragedies. These stories will bring other questions to mind. What were their personalities like? Who were the black sheep? Was anyone famous? Did anyone have unusual accomplishments? If she can provide you with photographs or documents, these can be used to inspire more questions, illustrate your story, or aid your research.

Members of your immediate family will be able to reference the times in your own life that you might have forgotten or were too young to register—aspects of your childhood such as your personality, ways of behaving, likes and dislikes, remarkable situations, and quirks. They may reveal the stories behind certain behavioral changes or

Just as most people love being photographed, many would appreciate your taking the time and interest to interview them about their lives. An interview not only reconnects you to the past, but also links you to those who live in the present.

sudden moves—situations that were previously hidden from you because you were too young to understand them at the time. Perhaps the reason your mother was distracted that particular year was because her sister's marriage was on the rocks. If you're feeling particularly bold, you can expand your research beyond your family to include interviews with your school friends, teachers, and neighbors.

Are you seeking to gain a different perspective of yourself? Interview your children—ask them what it's been like to have you as a mother or father.

Since you never know what will be expressed or revealed, do your best to keep an open mind when listening to others' comments. Do not judge what they say or how they express it, and you may be surprised by what you learn.

Why not create your own StoryBooth? Ask family and friends to interview each other. Involving others will raise questions you might never think to ask.

WRITER'S WORKSHOP

StoryBooth On October 23, 2003, a project called StoryCorps opened "StoryBooth," a small recording studio where people could interview friends and family at New York City's Grand Central Terminal, and soon it went nationwide.

Designed to inspire people to "record each others' stories in sound," the project resulted in many people conducting and recording interviews with family members, which with their permission were then housed at the StoryCorps Archive at the American Folklife Center at the Library of Congress. Samples of these interviews can be heard at their website (www. storycorps.net), along with guidelines on how to participate in the project or conduct your own interview.

Family Traits and Folklore

How many times have you heard someone say, "You're so much like your great-aunt?" Unfortunately, we don't get to meet all of our relatives, but that doesn't mean we don't share traits with them. Perhaps there's someone you have always identified with in your family, or someone who intrigued you as a child but whom you no longer see. Without access to this person, how can you possibly include them in your life story?

Looking for clues

As previously discussed, one route to finding out more is through interviews: you might not be able to talk directly to your great-aunt, but you may be able to talk to people who knew her. Plus, if you're lucky, she may have left some things behind that give you clues to her identity—photographs, letters, journals, postcards, books, or maybe a collection of jewelry. If you feel strongly intrigued by this person, try to figure out why. What gap does this specific person fill in your life? What answers do you expect her to provide?

Once you have gathered all the data you can on a particular individual, you can start to write about him or her. You may want to include the details of your search for information in your life story, including what your discoveries have meant to you and what you have eventually learned about yourself through them.

Using your imagination

If you are unable to collect much information through interviews, you have the option to speculate. Though this is your life story and you have a contract with the reader (and yourself) to tell the truth, this doesn't mean you can't put your imagination to use. As long as you come clean and admit that a certain passage is imagined, then you're keeping to this understanding. Maybe this person comes to you in a daydream and you envision her life as somehow parallel to yours. Or perhaps you take the one fact you have and run with it, creating a life around this one concrete piece of information. The things you imagine and choose to include will ultimately tell the reader many things about you.

Learn how to read what you find. What does someone's dress, posture, expression, handwriting, language, and word choice reveal about her and her social and historical context?

VOICES OF THE MASTERS

Mary Karr is a writer who uses family myths to great effect in her memoir, *The Liars' Club*. There are mythical stories that hover over families, which no one ever questions, but no one can absolutely swear are true. Such family myths are passed down through the generations and become part of a family's history. In *The Liars' Club,* Karr writes about the story behind the only photograph she has of her mother as a child. At two years old, Karr's mother was suffering from pneumonia and wasn't expected to live past midnight.

> *Nevertheless, about suppertime, Grandma got cheered by an idea…. If Charlie Marie was going to die, she said, then they'd better hurry up and get a picture of her for a keepsake…. So it was that my mother's fevered two-year-old self was stuffed in a bright red coat and propped out on the open front porch on a freezing January afternoon…. What made this story endure in our family is that it ends in a miracle. When the preacher arrived the next morning…ready to give comfort, Mother was sitting upright in bed…. Grandma liked to say it was the fresh air that healed her.*

While the reader can't know if the time outside did in fact cure Karr's mother, what is important is that Karr has the family myth of the "miracle" of her mother's survival—which reveals something of the grandmother's personality—to identify with the lone photograph of her mother as a child.

Sandra Cisneros's characters in *House on Mango Street* are based on real people from her life, but the book is written in the voice of Esperanza, an adolescent growing up in America. In the chapter "My Name," Esperanza reflects on what she shares with her great-grandmother.

> *It was my great-grandmother's name and now it is mine. She was a horse woman too, born like me in the Chinese year of the horse…. I would've liked to have known her, a wild horse of a woman, so wild she wouldn't marry. Until my great-grandfather threw a sack over her head and carried her off…. And the story goes she never forgave him. She looked out the window her whole life…. I have inherited her name, but I don't want to inherit her place by the window.*

Exploring Your Senses

One way to ensure that your writing comes alive is to employ your five senses—seeing, hearing, smelling, touching, and tasting. It's a surefire method of drawing your reader into the text so she's sharing the experience with you. Most of all, using sensory details helps to create a story your reader will remember.

Memory triggers

Keep in mind how one sense leads to or affects another. Have you ever smelled something so strong you could taste it? Has a scent ever prompted a memory of a conversation or a physical sensation? Is there a song you know that triggers a physical reaction in you?

Using sensory details will draw the reader in, helping them relate more fully to the scene. Just be careful not to include too much—you don't want to bore them with an endless list of observations when one or two might be more effective.

VOICES OF THE MASTERS

Esmeralda Santiago manages to include four of the five senses in this short extract from her memoir, entitled *When I was Puerto Rican*:

A green guava is sour and hard. You bite into it at its widest point, because it's easier to grasp with your teeth. You hear the skin, meat, and seeds crunching inside your head, while the inside of your mouth explodes in little spurts of sour.

WRITER'S WORKSHOP

Sensory exercises Try some of these exercises to practice your descriptive writing. They may inspire material worth including in your story.

- Describe one of the greatest meals you've ever eaten, including the aromas, the tastes and textures, and the way the food was presented. Depict the sounds around the table: the music, conversation, noise of silver against china, or even silence. How do these sensations create a mood?

- Describe a scene or scent that triggered a memory for you— someone's cologne, a special dish, or a location. Recall the memory and how it affected your present state. Now read the following poem by Claude McKay, and note how this visual scene takes him back in time.

> The Tropics in New York
> *Bananas ripe and green, and ginger-root*
> *Cocoa in pods and alligator pears,*
> *And tangerines and mangoes and grape fruit,*
> *Fit for the highest prize at parish fairs,*
>
> *Set in the window, bringing memories*
> *Of fruit-trees laden by low-singing rills,*
> *And dewy dawns, and mystical blue skies*
> *In benediction over nun-like hills.*
>
> *My eyes grew dim, and I could no more gaze;*
> *A wave of longing through my body swept,*
> *And, hungry for the old, familiar ways*
> *I turned aside and bowed my head and wept.*

When describing light, consider the difference between the blackness, the shadows, and the absence of light. What do your words mean?

- Visit an art museum. Look at and then describe a favorite photograph, sculpture, or painting. Try to demonstrate your emotional response to the piece without naming the emotion.

- Return to a moment when you felt extreme physical pleasure or pain. Slow down the clock and describe the sensations in detail, making it seem like the experience will never end.

- Read the following excerpt from "The Avenue Bearing the Initial of Christ into the New World" by Galway Kinnell. Envision the scene based on the sounds provided and described. Write your own poem that both includes and describes various sounds.

> pcheek pcheek pcheek pcheek pcheek
> They cry. The motherbirds thieve the air
> To appease them. A tug on the East River
> Blasts the bass-note of its passage, lifted
> From the infra-bass of the sea. A broom
> Swishes over the sidewalk like feet through leaves.
> Moves clack
>   clack
>   clack
> On a broken wheelrim. Ringing in its chains
> The New Star Laundry horse comes down the street
> Like a roofleak whucking in a pail….

- Describe light. How does a sunset differ from a sunrise, artificial light from natural? Where do shadows fall? In her essay "Seeing," Anne Dillard, an American essayist and memoirist, writes about fog:

> When you see fog move against a backdrop of deep pines, you don't see the fog itself, but streaks of clearness floating across the air in dark shreds.

- Describe silence. What do you hear when you close your eyes and plug your ears? Have you ever been surrounded by absolute silence? What was it like? Annie Dillard writes of silence in her essay "Teaching a Stone to Talk:"

> After a time you hear it: there is nothing there. There is nothing but those things only, those created objects, discrete, growing or holding, or swaying, being rained on or raining, held, flooding or ebbing, standing, or spread. You feel the world's word as a tension, a hum, a single chorused note everywhere the same. This is it: this hum is the silence.

Life Résumé

Since writing your life story involves evaluating your achievements and talents, it makes sense to put together a life résumé. Unlike your standard career résumé, your life résumé should also include more personal achievements and struggles. Use this exercise as an opportunity to review what's led you to the place you now occupy.

WRITER'S WORKSHOP

Creating your résumé Start with the headings listed below, and see what other ideas for headings come to mind. You can explore many more aspects of your life in this way. By the time your life résumé is complete, you'll have recorded countless memories and come up with numerous story ideas.

- **Work experience**—cover your jobs from babysitting and paper delivery to your most recent employment. Think back to all those summertime gigs and college jobs. Who did you work for, what was your first interview like, and who were your coworkers? What did you learn from these experiences? Which jobs did you like and which did you detest? (Unlike an employment résumé, your life résumé should include not just your greatest accomplishments and attributes, but also your failures.) Do you have one memorable experience for each job you held?

Annie Dillard writes about writing in The Writing Life:

"This morning, as on so many mornings, I lacked sufficient fuel for liftoff. I looked at the legal pad pages again. A new section must be begun in the book, and a place found to put it. I wrote four or five sentences on a gamble, smoked more to stimulate the brain or stop the heart, whichever came first, and reheated a fourth mug of coffee…."

- **Relationship experience**—include friendships, love and physically intimate relationships, familial relationships, and mentors. What years did these relationships span and what was your role in them? What were your strengths and weaknesses in each one? How did you grow in them and what did you bring from one relationship to the next?

- **Ailment experience**—the sicknesses and physical mishaps: every scraped knee, every bout of flu, operations, bee stings. What were your symptoms and reactions? How did you pass the time recuperating, and what was your cure? Did you lose hope at times? Consider your outlook on life and how it might have changed through an ailment.

Joan Didion writes about migraines in her essay "In Bed":

"Three, four, sometimes five times a month, I spend the day in bed with a migraine headache, insensible to the world around me. Almost every day of every month, between these attacks, I feel the sudden irritational irritation and flush of blood into the cerebral arteries which tell me that a migraine is on its way, and I take certain drugs to avert its arrival…. I fought migraine then, ignored the warnings it sent, went to school and later to work in spite of it, sat through lectures in Middle English and presentations to advertisers with involuntary tears running down the right side of my face, threw up in washrooms, stumbled home by instinct, emptied ice trays onto my bed and tried to freeze the pain in my right temple, wished only for a neurosurgeon who would do a lobotomy on house call, and cursed my imagination."

Life is a collection of firsts— your first kiss, first day of school, first job—and also resembles the patterns of a heartbeat: the peaks and slumps, the goals you've strived to achieve and the moments you've failed, and all the hard work in between.

- **Spaces inhabited**—where and with whom have you lived? What were the highlights of your time there or of the physical space itself?

- **Travel experience**—list places you have visited: repeated trips to your grandmother's house, summers camped by the lake, your honeymoon, visits overseas. What were the highlights of each journey, with whom did you share them, and who did you meet? Make notes of your first-time experiences, the disappointments, the times you got lost.

  Kate Wheeler writes about Bodh Gaya, in a book edited by Molly Emma Aitken, entitled Meeting the Buddha:

  Our destination was the Thai temple, past the far end of town, its delicate, fanciful gilt architecture bespeaking the never-ending elegance, the perfect gestures, of spiritual attainment. There, we would meditate for three weeks, awakened each morning by the thighbone trumpets as Himalayan monks performed meditative rituals; watching the parade of life from the safety of the high, iron gates. Beggars, dogs, cattle, and prancing little boys. Stunted ponies the size of Great Danes, pulling carts stuffed with whole families. Hindu holy men. Fresh faced Tibetans. Local folk on foot or bicycle…

- **Acquisitions**—can you think of any purchases that changed your life?

- **Hobbies**—what pastimes have you practiced, or objects have you collected, over the years?

- **Favorites**—favorite movies, songs, food, books, or clothes. What's the explanation behind each of these attachments? How has your taste evolved over the years? Who introduced you to your favorites?

- **Epiphanies**—have there been any grand realizations in your life—sudden moments when everything just clicked and fell into place?

- **Athletic accomplishments**—have you had any success in sports or games? If your preferred form of exercise is walking, where have you walked, with whom, and where did your thoughts roam? Have you ever run a marathon or played for a softball team?

- **Failures**—what goals have you failed to accomplish?

- **Successes**—what goals have you achieved?

- **Fears**—have you overcome any? Which fears have been with you for life?

School

You'll include school—kindergarten, elementary, junior high, high school, trade school, college or university—somewhere on your life résumé. By the time we're eighteen, most of us have spent at least twelve years in school. It's not only where we learned, but where we socialized, suffered, and excelled, were accepted and dismissed, felt challenged or bored, gave in to or fought off peer pressure, participated in trends or set our own, and sought to define our individuality. Look at how these experiences helped form the person you are today, even if you do not intend to focus on these early years.

Looking at your school days

Think back to kindergarten and your first day of school, if you can remember this far back. Were you happy to leave home or scared? Do you come from a large family or did you need to adjust to being around others? Were you outgoing or shy, the class clown or serious? Did you excel naturally or did you struggle? Who were your friends in these first few years and did the relationships last? Looking back, you may begin to see how character traits you developed early on at school have survived to the present day.

> Once you put yourself back in time, other memories will fall into place.

Consider specific school environments or situations and see if any memories come to mind—the lunchroom, gym, recess, the school bus, graduations, field trips. Try to visualize these experiences and then note down what you remember. Think about how the settings and activities changed as you progressed through the school years. What was it like to leave elementary school for junior high school? How did your interactions with others change? Do you recall your first crush, your first kiss? Did you ever attend a school dance? Were you a wallflower or a social butterfly, or somewhere in between? How did you feel walking down the hallway? Try to remember your body language, your social interactions, and your clothes. What were the social, cultural, and political climates of the time? Once you put yourself back in time, other memories will fall into place.

Graduation can be a monumental experience if you're the first in your family to do it, or it can be a stone on the path that sets you free to start a new life.

Revisiting the extremes

Revisit the extremes as you move on to high school. What were your greatest successes, your most humiliating experiences, your failures, and your fears? Many people look back on high school as the greatest time of their lives. How do you rate these years in comparison to what followed? Were there people who elicited a strong reaction from you—people you envied, adored, disliked, or feared?

Social cliques are a part of every school experience. Think about the groups of students you encountered and whether these groups changed as you moved through high school. Where did you fit in and how did this affect your interactions with other people? What was your place in the pecking order and was it where you wanted to be? Did you participate in any clubs or sports? Think about what role these activities had in your life and whether they affected your social life. What were your friendships like? Did they last, were they disrupted by moves, or did you drift through different social circles as you changed? Did you rebel at all?

Perhaps certain teachers had a great impact on your life. Who were they and why did they affect you so profoundly? What were your favorite subjects? Did they foreshadow your career? Were your post-high school goals clearly defined by you or your parents, or did you drift? If you went to college or university, remember what it was like to prepare for this experience—the applications, the campus visits, your parents' views, the deciding factors. What were your feelings on leaving home? Once you got to college, what was your reaction to this newfound liberty? Did a previously unknown self suddenly emerge? Again, revisit the extremes: your craziest moments, your points of crisis. How prepared were you for college life, and did these years prepare you for real life? All these questions will let you reflect on how your adult life began.

Consider how your school-age friends contributed to the making of the person you are today. Did you ever outgrow one set and seek another? Who do you remember most, and why?

VOICES OF THE MASTERS

Nathalie Sarraute uses memory to convey emotional experience in her memoir, entitled *Childhood*. In this excerpt she writes about a memory from her school days.

The mistress collects our papers. She is going to examine them, indicate the mistakes in red ink in the margin, then count them up and give the work a mark. Nothing can equal the fairness of the mark she will write under my name. It is justice itself, it is equity. It alone gives rise to that trace of approbation on the mistress's face when she looks at me. I am nothing other than what I have written. Nothing that I don't know, that people project on to me, that they foist on to me without my knowledge, as they are always doing there, outside, in my other life…

Rites of Passage

Rites of passage are events that act as bridges connecting one part of your life to the next, or that mark or celebrate a specific transition. They may be formal occasions such as graduations or bar/bat mitzvahs; other times they are private, intimate affairs, like when your dad took you on a boat trip and told you the facts of life. Your body can demonstrate these types of transitions, with the budding of adult teeth, the beginning of adolescence, or pregnancy. But no matter what the rite of passage, there are always steps that led you up to and through the threshold.

Chronicling the stages

Listing these steps one by one can help you construct a narrative for your journal, scrapbook, or memoir. Let's consider, for example, your wedding. What was the first step: the decision to marry, the buying of the ring, or the proposal? Once the commitment to wed was made, what were the various stages that led to the wedding day itself—making the public announcement, planning the event, deciding on the attire, choosing the guests, and so on? For the wedding day, most people have a photographer document each stage along the way—the rehearsal dinner, the dressing of the bride, her entrance, the ceremony, the kiss, the exit, and the ride to the reception. A wedding is an obvious example, but the chronological structure of most rites of passage makes for a pleasing narrative in words or images, depending upon your approach.

Perhaps the transition you wish to explore is not so public—maybe the act of falling in love, overcoming a phobia, or reentering society after rehabilitation. If you have kept a journal during this experience, so much the better; this will serve as a great point of reference, which we'll discuss in detail later on pages 62–65. If not, you must rely

upon your memory. What were you like before the change and at what point did you become aware that a change was even occurring? If you made the conscious decision to change, how, when, and why did this happen? Did life really alter after the experience, or was the moment symbolic of a great change that had been taking place over a longer period of time?

On the cusp of such a rite of passage as getting married, what was running through your mind? Recall your flashbacks and fears, your anticipations and dreams. Where did you envision your life in 15 years, and did your expectations come true?

Steps in life

Rites of passage can include birthdays, first jobs, or moving to another city or country. They can include momentous occasions such as buying a new house or car, or something simple like your first beer or your first grown-up movie. Perhaps your rite of passage involves becoming a member of a group or organization, like joining a sorority, a choral group, or an athletic team.

> It's important to pay attention to the symbols involved.

There will be some rites of passage that you cannot recall because you were too young to remember them, such as your baptism or bris. If this event has great significance for you, then it's possible to imagine it or to offer your own interpretation of it. What do you imagine actually occurred at this ceremony? What was the symbolic significance of the rite? Have you witnessed others going through the same ceremony? Can you incorporate their experience into your story? When writing about or depicting rituals, it's important to pay attention to the symbols involved. You may even want to research their origins, historical significance, and how they have been incorporated into the present world.

VOICES OF THE MASTERS

Rudyard Kipling, author of *Kim* and *The Jungle Book*, writes in his memoir, *Something of Myself,* about returning to India after his schooling in England.

> *So, at sixteen years and nine months, but looking four or five years older, and adorned with real whiskers which the scandalized Mother abolished within one hour of beholding, I found myself at Bombay where I was born, moving among sights and smells that made me deliver in the vernacular sentences whose meaning I knew not. Other Indian-born boys have told me how the same thing happened to them.*
>
> *There were yet three or four days' rail to Lahore, where my people lived. After these, my English years fell away, nor ever, I think, came back in full strength.*

Not only do we get a sense of how long Kipling has been gone from home, but we are also made to realize the importance of his return, which represents the end of a transitory phase in his life and therefore a rite of passage for him, virtually erasing the ten years he spent away.

Work and Career

By retirement, most people have had numerous jobs, including first jobs as babysitter, grocery clerk, mover, lawn cutter, or newspaper carrier. Some people work all their lives toward one specific goal, knowing from the outset what they were meant to do. Others meander, changing jobs like socks, either finding satisfaction in none, or knowing their passion for living resides outside of their career. Many writers live like this, taking on jobs to support their craft, while feeling more defined by their writing than by what pays the bills. Regardless of whether your work has led you to the top of the food chain at a major corporation, behind the counter at a coffee shop, around the world, through the forests at your local park, or in the kitchen at home, it's a story that deserves to be told.

VOICES OF THE MASTERS

David Sedaris, humorist and essay writer, illustrates one of many possible approaches to writing about work. He is able to turn the most mundane experience into a hilarious piece of writing. In *Me Talk Pretty One Day,* he includes an essay entitled "The Great Leap Forward," in which we meet the fellow movers who carried furniture

up and down flights of stairs with him: Patrick, "a card-carrying communist…[who] hated being referred to as the boss…. One look at his teeth, and you could understand his crusade for universal health care…. A convicted murderer named Richie, who, at six feet four and close to 350 pounds, was a poster boy for both the moving industry and the failure of the criminal rehabilitation system." Sedaris's willingness to reflect honestly upon his own role is partly what makes him so funny. Later in the essay he writes:

> *Moving heavy objects allowed me to feel manly in the eyes of other men. With the women it didn't matter, but I enjoyed subtly intimidating the guys with bad backs who thought they were helping out by telling us how to pack the truck. The thinking was that because we were furniture movers, we obviously weren't too bright. In addition to being strong and stupid, we were also thought of as dangerous. It might have been an old story to Patrick and the others, but I got a kick out of being mistaken as volatile. All I had to do was throw down my dolly with a little extra force, and a bossy customer would say, "Let's all calm down and try to work this out."*

VOICES OF THE MASTERS

Richard Selzer, a practicing surgeon, employs a variety of metaphors for the knife, and for the surgeon who uses it, in his essay "The Knife" in *Mortal Lessons: Notes on the Art of Surgery*. His extensive use of detail draws the reader into the situation. In this extract, he compares the surgeon to a traveler:

But mostly you are a traveler in a dangerous country, advancing into the moist and jungly cleft your hands have made. Eyes and ears are all shuttered from the land you left behind; mind empties itself of all other thought. You are the root of groping fingers. It is a fine hour for the fingers, their sense of touch so enhanced. The blind man must know this feeling. Oh, there is risk everywhere. One goes lightly. The spleen. No! No! Do not touch the spleen that lurks below the left leaf of the diaphragm, a manta ray in the coral cave, its bloody tongue protruding.

One poke and it might rupture, exploding with sudden hemorrhage. The filmy omentum must not be torn, the intestine scraped or denuded. The hand finds the liver, palms it, fingers running along its sharp lower edge, admiring….

Even though Selzer uses the second person, it is he who is the "traveler in a dangerous country," exploring the guts and cavity of his patients' bodies, each one a new and dangerous journey.

Do you ascribe your achievements in the workplace to education and hard work, or have you simply been lucky? How has what you do for a living affected the person you are?

Reflecting on your job

Your attitude toward the job you are describing will partly determine the tone of your writing— humorous, serious, tense, contented, or angry. Reflect on the various jobs you have had. Note how these positions defined you, what you learned, who you met, and what your feelings were of the work itself and the workplace environment. What got you to where you are now—was it education, hard work, luck, connections, or mistakes? Over the years, what's gotten you through the workday—dedication, a sense of humor, relationships, a sense of accomplishment, or the thought of heading out the door at the end of the day and returning home? Have there been times in your life when home has been a place you'd rather avoid and work has provided a sanctuary?

Family Photographs

Photographs make great memory triggers and can be so powerful that the picture sometimes replaces the memory itself. What better way to recall the physical attributes of yourself when younger, or one of your life story's characters, than to have a photograph in front of you? Sometimes your memories are tucked just beneath the surface and need some kind of stimulus to release them. The décor of your family's living room in 1957 might escape you, but with that photograph of your sister by the Christmas tree, you can suddenly recall the grandfather clock that never ticked or the rocking chair by the window where you spent hours reading books while the neighborhood children played outside.

VOICES OF THE MASTERS

This photograph, which inspired the passage on the right, shows the bar in my grandmother's house. The people are my sister, mother, aunt, cousin, and uncle.

Every family gathering was staged at Dziadzia's bar.

My grandfather Dziadzia built a bar before he died. It's a beautiful bar with wood panels the color of whiskey on the front and red Formica on the surface. It's approximately twelve feet long and L-shaped with a rounded curve at the corner and rises to the height that enables most adults to lean on an elbow while standing.

Its back bar was where the alcohol was stored—bottles of Absolut, Johnny Walker, Crown Royal, and Jack Daniels. Always nearby was a cooler jammed with cold beer and on the bar, pastel colored plastic bowls filled with chips and dips. Uncle Joe bought glasses with each adult's initial—J, K, F, H, and C—so that no one would mistakenly sip the cocktail of another. The adults drank. As kids, we sat at the bar sipping soda, sometimes sneaking a lick of the forbidden juice, or sucking a mouthful of foam from a glass of freshly poured beer. Once I was tall enough, I found my way behind the counter.

Jogging your memory

As the years go by, your fifteenth birthday might as well have been your fourteenth, until you bring out the family album to compare the two, and only then do you remember that your fourteenth was a dull affair in a pizza parlor while your fifteenth had your best friend fainting just as the cake and candles arrived. Pictures can also resurrect the people you might have forgotten, the small details of significant events, or even the memories you would have rather left in the past. For a journal or scrapbook, photographs might well be an essential part of your display. Since memoirs and personal essays don't often incorporate imagery, pictures in these genres are best used as tools to jog your memory.

Using an image

An image records a moment in time, one so small you might have forgotten it completely if it hadn't been captured in a photograph. Pull out your old albums and look for people or moments you might have missed. Study facial expressions and body language and the way in which people are captured interacting with their environment, with each other, and with the person behind the camera. Try writing about one of these moments, and see what story comes up from the mix.

Although photographs capture a fraction of a second, a specific moment in time, they also tend to illustrate certain moods, dynamics, character traits, and relationships. as author Tim Guest (right) found.

VOICES OF THE MASTERS

Tim Guest, a British writer, includes photographs from his childhood in his memoir *My Life in Orange* to illustrate his experience of growing up in a commune. The final page shows a passport picture of the author as a baby with his parents.

On the last page of my father's photo album is an early passport snapshot blown up six inches wide so that the family unit can be seen more clearly. There we are, the three of us, crammed into a photo booth not long after I was born. I'm looking off to one side, checking out something to the right of the frame. My mother is staring up to the left: her eyes are already moving away. My father is looking straight at the camera so that now, across my whole lifetime, I can look him in the eye…. The thing that strikes me now about the photo is that no one is looking at anyone else. We've already started on our own particular journeys. We are together, but already alone.

As I look at this photo…I want to take something of my heart and push it through the glossy paper, through the lens of the camera and back in time. I want to tell them I'll be OK…. I want to wish them luck for what is coming.

Tim Guest and his parents

Public Photographs

Images used to illustrate or inspire writings don't have to be from the family album. We're surrounded by pictures and have easy access to images from the past. Making use of photographs that depict local or world events is a good way to give your story context. These photographs can offer a picture of the greater setting that surrounds your own experience—the historical, cultural, political, and social contexts that might help you illustrate or illuminate your text.

Turning to the Media

You can clip articles on your local country fair, a war, or the death of your favorite performer. If you are an activist, you might search for images of the various demonstrations you've attended; if you're a music fan, you can look for coverage of when your favorite musician came to town. If you have a loved one in a war overseas, you have probably already spent a lot of time poring over newspapers and magazines, looking for pictures that give you hints of what he or she might be going through.

Using images from the past

Perhaps a world event coincides with a particular experience that you want to write about. You might even use a well-documented public occasion to express your own feelings, such as a sense of personal triumph or accomplishment. You can't always illustrate a mental breakthrough, and might not always have a camera on hand to document a personal event, but this doesn't mean that you can't include images to help convey your message. For example, when the American astronaut Neil Armstrong first walked on the moon on July 21, 1969, many people agreed that it was indeed "one small step for man, but one giant leap for mankind."

Neil Armstrong made a solid leap for all of mankind. His achievement fueled the imaginations and aspirations of many, who saw that what was once considered impossible could indeed be done.

What was going through the minds of Hillary and Norgay when they reached the summit of Mount Everest? Not many of us have climbed Mount Everest but anyone who has struggled can imagine the sense of achievement they experienced at the summit.

While the personal event that you wish to convey may or may not be a "giant leap for mankind," it might have inspired a similar sensation in you, or may have played an equally significant role in your life. If you're not interested in space travel, you might choose to include images of another milestone, such as Edmund Hillary and Tenzing Norgay's conquest of Mount Everest in 1953.

> ### There are unlimited numbers of well-photographed world or local events.

Of course, there are many other such events that might depict triumph: an election won by your favorite candidate, the end of a war, your favorite author winning a prize, or a victory by your chosen sports team. Or you might wish to illustrate an emotion other than that experienced with success.

There are unlimited numbers of well-photographed world or local events that you could use to represent personal feelings of hope, struggle, love, failure, loss, reunion, or discovery. You might select photographs that also illustrate your work, hobbies, passions, or relationships—the meanings you can attach to an image are limitless, and can give your life story an added dimension.

If you are writing about a place, either to which you've traveled or where you live, you might collect images from books, papers, and magazines, images that span an extensive period of time. Such images can be sprinkled throughout your text, be used to inspire writings, or assembled into a collage. Found imagery can also be used to reveal fantasies or dreams; for example, using a picture of King Kong to illustrate how you hope to crush your competition, or an image taken underwater to show how you might wish to isolate yourself from whatever chaos you are experiencing, and escape.

Old Journals and Letters

What material could better aid your research than your own writings from the past? Whether journals, notes, or letters, nothing can better help you access the details, the emotions, or the essence of the moment than text you wrote yourself. If you haven't kept journals, then perhaps you have drafts of letters; and if not letters, then e-mail messages. Did you keep up a correspondence while experiencing personal turmoil or success? See if you still have these exchanges. If you no longer have e-mails or letters, maybe your friend has them and will share them with you.

VOICES OF THE MASTERS

I made the following journal entries during my trek through the Annapurna region of the Himalayas. With some work, they could be used as the basis of a chapter in my life story.

Karen Ulrich

Tirkhe, March 24, 1994

Yesterday a man led us to the old temple here and took us inside. Come to find it's about 400 years old. Incredible. The paintings peel off the walls as stones shift. It's decayed. I guess it's been abandoned for twelve years, since the lama died, and they say he passed like a Buddha—in sitting posture for three days, until slowly his face caved in, black fell from one nostril, white from the other. People came to worship and an opening formed in the top of his skull. Now the temple is decayed and left to nature, which I guess isn't so bad.

I don't feel like I have much to write about. I haven't been thinking about much. The trekking requires all focus on one foot in front of the other.

The Annapurna region of the Himalayas—a world away from the madness of New York. Stepping out of your habitual environment can bring insight to your memoir writing because it gives you useful distance on your life back home.

Kagbeni, March 27

> *[I succumbed to] the intense meditation one falls into while walking all day. He called it "riverbed fever," walking along [the Kali Gandaki River gorge] seeing the same riverbed, all day long. Not that I mind. It's a feeling that carries me through each day and night.*

Tatopani, beginning of April

> *Seeing how people resemble their environment here really makes me wonder what we look like in New York. In Kagbeni, the lines on people's faces are like folds in the earth. In Jharkot this man stood before us with a baby on his back, veins running along his face, across his mountainous cheekbones.... I can see the Buddha in him sitting tall, spine erect like a mountain. Each step a mantra; Om mani padme hum literally passes through the lips of my mind as I move each foot forward.*

Pokhara, April 6

I felt I couldn't be bothered by all the little annoyances, because it took me three weeks to obtain this head and I wasn't going to lose it so easily over a trivial nothing…and now these three weeks are a great memory. I just hope that each time I dip into the pool of my past, I am able to gain a bit of love when I need it. It's still so overwhelming to think of what these weeks were about. As the days pass, I'll realize more and more what a jewel I held for some time.

Keeping a Daily Journal

If you have never kept a daily journal and wish you had, there's no better time to start than now. Daily journals can serve many purposes and, as we have seen, make excellent resources when you are looking for writing material later on.

Recording your raw response

The difference between a journal that you share with family and friends (in essence, a polished version of your daily journal) and a memoir is that the latter takes a more narrative form, so do not mistake your journal for your final project, if a memoir is what you intend to write. Daily journal entries are best written up immediately following the experience you are writing about; memoirs require a lot of thought and craft, and therefore are not the place to record your raw response to an experience. However, this raw response can serve your research by bringing you back to the situation at hand, when the experience has long passed.

> Your journal has an endless capacity to listen.

Since writing is a form of communication, the act of writing can help you figure things out, just as if you were talking to a friend. It's a great way to process information when you are overwhelmed by a life full of activity or feeling. Are you going through difficult times, but feel you've relied on friends or family too much? Write. Your journal has an endless capacity to listen, and when you've written all you can, chances are you'll feel a lot better. You can later use these writings in your life story, whether that takes the form of a journal, scrapbook, or memoir.

From politicians and great thinkers to athletes, pre-adolescent girls, and expectant mothers and dads—many people have found diaries are the perfect place to document their development.

Your journal is also an excellent place to write letters you'll never send—a place to vent and let go of your feelings without having to suffer the consequences of hurting or offending someone. Again you may decide to use those letters later on in your life story.

If you are traveling, what better way to document your trip than in your daily journal? Photographs don't capture your inner story or mood the way writing in the privacy of your own journal can. It's also a great place to store your ephemera while on the road. Here you can collect detailed information on the food you ate, the people you met, what you saw and learned, the places you stayed, your dreams, the places you loved or hated, and your emotional reactions to the experience. Any of these elements may later find a place in your life story.

What to record

It's a good idea to document the steps of an experience as you go through them, whether it's the beginning or ending of a relationship, starting a new job, returning to school, having a baby, relocating, or embarking on a new life. Human memory is a notoriously imperfect facility, requiring as much back-up as possible. Your thoughts and feelings continually adapt to your changing circumstances and, if you don't record your thought processes as you experience them, your mind will be tempted to edit your past and deliver a smoothed-over version of how things really were.

You may want to carry a little pocket notebook to record ideas as they come to mind (quick, before you lose them!), document overheard snippets of conversation, write down favorite words, or record your immediate reactions to movies, museum exhibits, and books.

Since writing your life story involves a great deal of soul searching, think about keeping a journal to

record your experience of writing. What does it feel like to unearth your past, to revisit old settings, and to contemplate the various places you've been? Write these things down as you're going through them and you'll be surprised by how this fuels both your creativity and your ability to remember events from your past.

> ### While researching your life story, you'll learn of old secrets.

While researching your life story, you'll learn of old secrets, remember what's long been forgotten, uncover the real motives or truths behind the actions of others, and confront decisions you have made. Document this emotional journey and you might find that it, too, has a place in your life story.

Snaps like these perfectly capture outward appearances, but a travel journal allows you the freedom to explore beneath the surface. Note your impressions and discoveries while they're still fresh in your mind, and you'll have an invaluable resource to plunder later.

Ephemera

Ephemera are those everyday items, often made from card or paper, that by their nature have only temporary use or importance, like theater programs, pamphlets, notices, tickets, and so on. Since they relate to a specific moment in time, which is what you are often seeking to portray when writing, why not use these mementos to jog your memory?

Getting inspiration

If you already have a collection of ephemera, what kind of things have you saved? Is your collection specific, such as train or plane tickets, concert or movie tickets, or matchbooks? If so, then you already have a story behind each ticket, and you might let your collection guide the writing of your life story. Perhaps you want to write your life story in terms of movies, beginning with the first movie you ever saw and the effect it had on you, and then recording or exploring every movie you've seen since. What was going on in your life and in the world at the time when you first viewed particular movies? Did you identify with the subject or the characters? The same could be done for concerts, plays, musicals, or museum exhibits, and you can display your ephemera alongside your story.

Perhaps you collect more unusual items, such as foreign newspapers or magazines, product labels, bar coasters, maps, or advertisements, each with its own story to tell. Maybe in anticipation of your trip to Mexico you purchased Mexican newspapers and magazines to help you master the language and learn something of the culture. What did you learn and how did this research affect your expectations?

Did it contrast with the reality of the place once you arrived? Or perhaps you collected product labels on your trip across Asia, some depicting the foods you loved, others whose design pleased or intrigued you, and some because you found the products unusual. You can use these labels to inspire memories or to illustrate your experiences.

For those who hang onto mementoes that have a more personal story behind them, such as party invitations, birth notices, report cards, wedding announcements, or greeting cards, the story behind

Nothing tells a life story like a heavily stamped passport or a collection of tickets to illustrate where you've been.

each is pretty clear unless the item is so old you cannot recall why you kept it; in this case, you might need to conduct some additional research to fill in the gaps. These items might help you reflect on how a person, or your relationship with him or her, has changed over the years or they might mark life-changing events. In the third part of the book (see pages 138–185), we'll look at how you can display or manipulate your ephemera to best suit your life story project.

> Old postcards might suggest some kind of mystery you want to solve.

Postcards, either those you have collected from places you have visited or those you have been sent, can inspire stories or, in the case of those received, can tell your reader something about your relationship with the sender. Old postcards, which belonged to a parent or grandparent, might tell you things you didn't know, or suggest some kind of mystery you might want to imagine or solve. You can also collect postcards from flea markets and use them to suggest, represent, or symbolize an aspect of your life.

The various images and graphics on postcards, leaflets and pamphlets, old gift cards, and matchbooks can provide your reader with visual clues to your life story.

Dreams

Dreams have inspired numerous creations—movies, poems, paintings, plays, and books. As the creative outlet for your subconscious, they certainly deserve some attention, but remembering dreams requires practice. By keeping a dream book beside your bed and developing a habit of writing down whatever you recall upon waking, you'll soon find yourself remembering more about your dreams. You never know where you're going to find your story, so you should keep track of every dream you can.

Finding a place for your dreams

Have you ever woken in a panic from a nightmare when it seemed that everything in your life was fine? Take a closer look at disturbing dreams and you may discover that something is bothering you that you have chosen to ignore. Exposing your subconscious and including your dreams in your life story is an unusual way to show the reader what you were going through at the time, rather than simply recounting your state of mind. If the reader gets to read your dreams, then she bears witness to your inner life.

> Disturbing dreams may lead you to discover that something is bothering you.

You may have had dreams that brought you pleasure, and some so strange you can't believe you had the potential to create such a scenario in your mind. You may have been so affected by what you dreamt that it took a while for you to realize it wasn't reality. What was your most bizarre dream? What made it so strange? Ask yourself questions about your dreams. Did you ever have a recurring dream when you were a child? What nighttime scenarios left you longing and what were you longing for? Have you ever been embarrassed by your dreams or what you said or thought in them? Do you have recurring characters in your dreams? Who stands out the most? Write these dreams and details down and use them to add important dimensions to your life story.

In sleep the body rests, but the mind is active, visiting places you wouldn't dare to go during daylight, or struggling to resolve the issues you didn't complete before sleep.

VOICES OF THE MASTERS

Po Chu-I, a poet and government official in the 9th century China, wrote the following poem when he was 70 years old. Known for the simplicity of his writing, he mainly produced ballads and satire. In the poem, dreaming is presented as an opportunity for a second life; the sleeping mind succeeds where the body isn't able to. Like Po Chu-I, you can contrast your dreams with the reality of your waking life to illustrate a conflict or desire.

A Dream of Mountaineering

> *At night, in my dream, I stoutly climbed a mountain,*
> *Going out alone with my staff of holly-wood.*
> *A thousand crags, a hundred hundred valleys—*
> *In my dream-journey none were unexplored*
> *And all the while my feet never grew tired*
> *And my step was as strong as in my young days.*
> *Can it be that when the mind travels backward*
> *The body also returns to its old state?*
> *And can it be, as between body and soul,*
> *That the body may languish, while the soul is still strong?*
>
> *Soul and body—both are vanities;*
> *Dreaming and walking—both alike unreal.*
> *In the day my feet are palsied and tottering;*
> *In the night my steps go striding over the hills.*
> *As day and night are divided in equal parts—*
> *Between the two, I get as much as I lose.*

PO CHU-I (722–846), *translated by Arthur Waley*

Mountains, a great source of mystery, have housed demons and gods and have inspired the desire to conquer their peaks.

Music

There are many ways in which you can use music to aid the development of your life story. It can help inspire memories, serve as a time line, set a tone or mood, illustrate your feelings, paint a picture of the times, or even be the subject of your writing.

Triggering memories

Try listening to music from the time period you are writing about. Not only does this help bring you back to the mood of the time, but it can also trigger memories—the song that was a hit at your school dance, the tune that marks a friend or lover's departure, your wedding song, or the music that got you through a difficult time. Listening to music from another period in your life, especially if it's music you don't listen to much any more, will bring that time back to the surface and bring you closer to the feelings you experienced then.

Music to set the time

To use music as a time line, you can start by making a list of the musicians who shared the different phases of your life, beginning with the first single or album that you bought or with the first musicians you heard on the radio.

What was the culture that enveloped or inspired these songs? How, and when, did your taste in music change? Who shared your taste at each particular period and how did your relationships change along with your musical preferences? Perhaps certain people in your life introduced you to new music: who were they? The answers to any of these questions might provide you with a situation or relationship you could write about. Creating a musical time line may even help you structure your story.

In his essay, "When the Negro Was in Vogue," Langston Hughes recalls how Manhattan's Black Renaissance in the 1920s changed course when, "some of the owners of Harlem clubs, delighted at the flood of white patronage, made the grievous error of barring their own race, after the manner of the famous Cotton Club." He recalls the music scene in Harlem—not just the musicians and their acts, but the frustrations the Harlem residents experienced as they were excluded from the Harlem Renaissance they had helped create. They lost not only their clubs to the affluent whites but also their musicians.

The music played at the Cotton Club in its heyday, like the club itself, belongs to a bygone era. Music has enormous power to evoke a mood and stimulate memory. What songs do you associate with different periods of your life?

VOICES OF THE MASTERS

Langston Hughes describes the performance of Gladys Bentley in this passage to give the reader a sense of the vibrancy of Harlem in the 1920s.

Gladys Bentley, who was something worth discovering in those days, before she got famous, acquired an accompanist, specially written material, and conscious vulgarity. But for two or three amazing years, Miss Bentley sat, and played a big piano all night long, literally all night, without stopping—singing songs like "The St. James Infirmary," from ten in the evening until dawn, with scarcely a break between the notes, sliding from one song to another, with a powerful and continuous underbeat of jungle rhythm. Miss Bentley was an amazing exhibition of musical energy—a large, dark, masculine lady, whose feet pounded the floor while her fingers pounded the keyboard—a perfect piece of African sculpture, animated by her own rhythm.

Langston Hughes made enormous artistic contributions to the Harlem Renaissance. In his essay "The Negro Artist and the Racial Mountain," first published in The Nation*, Hughes wrote, "An artist must be free to choose what he does, certainly, but he must also never be afraid to do what he must choose."*

Music often brings us together, serving as an umbrella for various political, social, racial, or cultural movements.

> ## Maybe you strongly identified with the lyrics of a song.

Depending upon the time you're describing, you may choose to use music as a background to your story, to illustrate the mood of the time, social or cultural tensions, or personal conflicts. Music also separates one generation from the next, and you may want to use it to define your generation. Maybe you strongly identified with the lyrics of a song at a particular point of your life. If so, you might choose to use an excerpt from a song within your story. Whatever your relationship with music, there are numerous ways you can use it to inspire or illustrate certain aspects of your life, whether it's to extract an emotion or memory, link characters together, or depict a specific scene.

Inspirations

There are many ways you can incorporate the people and places that have inspired or influenced you into your life story. You might choose to do so by making the person or the place a main character in your story, as Anatole Broyard did with New York in his memoir, *Kafka Was the Rage* (see page 30) or as Vivian Gornick did with her mother and the building full of women in her memoir, *Fierce Attachments* (see page 129). In a scrapbook or journal you might consider dedicating pages to these people or places, complete with illustrations or photographs or quotations to show what you have learned from them. Whatever format you choose, you should consider paying respect to those who helped make you.

Ways of giving credit

If you have a favorite author or visual artist, you might begin your homage by trying to mimic his or her work. Since it takes time to find your own voice, you can try on the voices of others, until you create your own. Many great artists began by copying their masters; it's an excellent way to learn a craft. You might even acknowledge your source of inspiration by incorporating the person's name or the title of his or her work into your own title.

Just as with music, you could create a timeline based on people who influenced your development. Who were the various role models in your life and how did they contribute to your growth or change? Perhaps one particular athletic coach helped you reach what you thought were unattainable goals. Perhaps there were teachers along the way who helped you recognize or develop specific talents. In your scrapbook or journal, you might consider including "before" and "after" samples of your work, while recording the process you engaged in. Who were you before you encountered these people and how did you change as a result of their influence?

Who helped you realize your natural abilities and talents, and how exactly did she do it? Was there a teacher who encouraged you to write, a coach who helped you recognize your athletic potential, a spiritual leader who knew your capacity to reach others, or an instructor who taught you how to maximize your potential as a leader?

VOICES OF THE MASTERS

The Dalai Lama, in his autobiography *Freedom in Exile,* writes about his mother in Tibet, whose kindness clearly inspired the development of his own compassion.

My mother was undoubtedly one of the kindest people I have ever known. She was truly wonderful and was loved, I am quite certain, by all who knew her. She was very compassionate. Once, I remember being told, there was a terrible famine in nearby China. As a result, many poor Chinese people were driven over the border in search of food. One day, a couple appeared at our door, carrying in their arms a dead child. They begged my mother for food, which she readily gave them. Then she pointed at their child and asked whether they wanted help to bury it. When they had caught her meaning, they shook their heads and made clear that they intended to eat it. My mother was horrified and at once invited them in and emptied the entire contents of the larder before regretfully sending them on their way. Even it if meant giving away the family's own food so that we ourselves went hungry, she never let any beggars go empty-handed.

Focus on the politicians, inspirational leaders such as Martin Luther King (above), inventors, thinkers, and artists who helped create the world you inhabit, and appreciate, today.

The current Dalai Lama, born in 1935, writes to make Buddhism accessible to Western readers and, as the exiled leader of Tibet, to campaign for that country's independence. He was awarded the Nobel Peace Prize in 1989.

You can consider how individuals inspired you to change.

Perhaps you had role models who weren't accessible—activists, politicians, athletes, performers, or artists. You can still consider how these individuals inspired you to change. You may have been greatly influenced by a spiritual leader, for instance, who you've never met, but whose teachings you have studied. You might include excerpts of his or her work, your response to these excerpts, or an explanation of how these teachings inspired a change in you and your actions over time. You might even write a letter to your mentor, describing just how he or she influenced you. What were the specific actions, thoughts, or accomplishments that made you take notice of this person and what was your life like before this individual changed you?

Secrets

If you are writing your life story solely for yourself, you don't need to worry about exposing secrets—you can write your deepest, darkest thoughts and reveal all you want about someone or something, because the audience will not extend beyond you. However, if you plan to share your life story with others, then you need to consider just how much you should reveal, and how and when it might be appropriate to tell or keep secrets.

Revealing yourself

Writing a life story is tricky, not only because it means writing about others but also because you need to consider how much of yourself you are willing to lay on the line. The best memoirs rely on the honesty of the writer—how much he is willing to reveal and how deep he is willing to dig into the ground that buries his past.

> The best memoirs rely on the honesty of the writer.

How to handle your secrets

Sometimes the muscles that guard history are tight and need to be loosened or stretched. The exercises in the Writer's Workshop opposite will help you get used to the idea of committing secrets to the page and exposing yourself to scrutiny in a way that you wouldn't normally consider. Try to be as truthful with yourself as possible.

Obviously, a terrible act or thought committed at the age of five usually loses its potential to harm or expose as the years move on. However, sometimes there are fantasies or thoughts, or aspects of our personality that once seemed so horrific, they became permanently difficult to reveal. If this is occurring, try to find a way to

incorporate the experience into your life story. Look into what's holding you back, whose judgments you fear, or whom you think might abandon you for such thoughts.

The same can be said for family secrets. Now that you are writing your life story, it's time for you to decide how much of this is true. Only you can anticipate how you might feel upon releasing the information that's been weighing you down. Consider how your story might aid the future generations of your family by providing them with explanations for strange personalities, relationships, or quirks. But, also consider the risks.

When writing your life story, it may take time to establish a comfortable relationship with the truth. Only you can determine how much is enough or too much.

WRITER'S WORKSHOP

Coming to terms with exposure Be sure to keep your responses to these exercises to yourself. They are designed to test your limits and make you aware of where your comfort zone lies. The final exercise will help you identify your secrets, or rather, the subjects you are likely to feel uncomfortable exploring in your memoir.

- Write down someone else's secret, something you swore you would take to the grave.

- Write about a fantasy, sexual or otherwise, something you would normally feel embarrassed to reveal.

- Select someone close to you and write about your unexpressed feelings toward him or her.

- Write a letter to someone close to you (don't send it!), revealing something you would never tell.

- Make a list of guilt-ridden doubts.

- Make a list of all the people you feel you need to protect and explain why you need to protect them and what you need to protect them from.

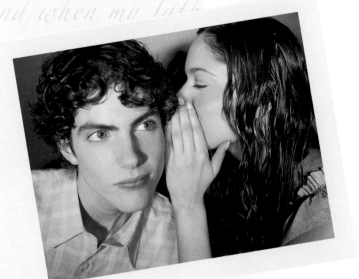

Secrets bring us closer to others, but they can also drive relationships apart. Consider why you decided not to disclose the thoughts, feelings, experiences, and/or ideas that you chose to keep to yourself.

Facing the fear

When writing your life story, you will undoubtedly be forced to confront situations or issues that make you uncomfortable; this is a part of the process. What you need to decide, based on the exercises above, is how many of these situations you want to include in your memoir.

Never let fear stop you from writing. You might want to reveal one thought at a time, on separate journal pages, if this is what it takes to make you feel you aren't revealing too much, too fast. In this way you can ration the amount that you feel you are revealing about yourself.

If this doesn't work, you may need to let more time pass. The further an experience is in the past, the less weight you and others will give it. And it's worth noting that everyone recalls shared experiences differently, so chances are that you could write about an event so that it's unrecognizable to the people involved—that is, if they haven't already forgotten about it. If this still doesn't seem right, then you need to wait until the person you fear hurting has passed from your life.

Remember it's your life story, no one else's. Your life experience is your property, and you should treat it as such: with honor, respect, and honesty.

Objects

Just like photographs, objects—from heirlooms to childhood toys, wedding gowns to pieces of furniture, a favorite blanket or cup—make excellent memory triggers. Have you held on to things from the past? If so, see if you can find items from the past that you associate with specific times, feelings, or events. If you spend time with these items, you might be surprised to find what they bring back.

The role of objects in your life

Even if you can't find an object from your past, try to recall one that was a significant part of your life. Then explore the role this object played and what it meant to you—the bicycle or car that brought you freedom, the doll that comforted you when you felt sad, the ball you spent hours bouncing from the stoop to alleviate your boredom. The list of possible items is limitless.

Consider the relationships that revolved around objects—those with whom you rode your bike, drove around with, or loved in your car. What role did the object play and how might the relationship have been different if this object didn't exist? If the objects of your choice are a bit quirky, such as paraphernalia from a favorite childhood TV show, then you might even look into who shares your passion, or explore what inspired your collection and how you acquired such goods.

Gifts are often significant for how they might symbolize the relationship between the giver and receiver. Think of your most favorite, most treasured, most hurtful, most confused, or most inexplicable gift. Did your receiving (or giving) this object alter, improve or weaken your relationship in any way?

Remember your first bicycle ride: the moment your pedaling gained momentum; what it felt like to venture away from home; the wind in your hair; the sinking of your belly as you descended that long-forgotten hill at breakneck speed.

VOICES OF THE MASTERS

Nathalie Sarraute's memoir, *Childhood*, is not only beautifully written and emotionally rich, but is also a fascinating exercise in exploring memory. A French novelist who was born in Russia, Sarraute tries to extract meaning from her past throughout her memoir, including the isolation she experienced as a result of strained relationships with her mother and father, who separated when she was young.

In the following excerpt she remembers a book her father gave her, and the relationship she had to a particular page.

I have been given a big bound book, a very thin one, which I love looking through. I enjoy listening when they read me what is written opposite the pictures…but careful!—we're getting to that picture, it frightens me, it's horrible…a very thin man with a long, pointed nose, dressed in a bright green frockcoat with floating tails, is brandishing a pair of open scissors, he's going to cut into the flesh, blood is going to flow…. "I can't look at it, it must go…." "Would you like us to tear out the page?" "That would be a pity, it's such a beautiful book." "Well, then, we'll hide that picture…. We'll stick the pages together." Now I don't see it any more, but I know that it's still there, shut in…here it is, approaching, hidden here, where the page gets thicker…. I have to turn the pages very quickly, I have to pass over this one before it has time to alight in me, to become embedded…it has already begun to take shape, those scissors cutting into the flesh, those big drops of blood…but that's it now, we've passed it, it's eclipsed by the next picture.

What's interesting here is that the passage reveals the author's emotional experience, perhaps in relation to her parents—not just her fear of the man in the book. The object allows her to access this emotion.

Use objects as a means of access

Make a list of the objects you have formed attachments to over the years and consider what these objects have done for you, what gaps they filled in your life, or what emotions they enabled you to feel. Use these objects, as Sarraute did, to access what might not initially seem clear to you. Whether used to access forgotten memories, unknown needs, or hidden emotions, objects from your past can be used as tools to uncover aspects of your life story.

If you find yourself with a collection of objects that are difficult to part with, then you might begin with asking yourself why. How do you foresee your life without them, and what was occurring in your life when this collection began? The answer to the latter question might provide some insight on what you were looking to mask or gain. Or, perhaps you wish to explore the possessions of another, in your life story—like the jewelry collection you inherited from your grandmother, beginning with the origins of the various pieces and what they meant to her.

The Body

Your body is a great source of information, since its physical changes have been the cause of numerous experiences and conflicts. Adolescence, accidents, ailments, addictions, weight loss and gain, disease, exercise, sex, birth, recovery, and the signs of aging—all of these transformations involve some change within the body, but the experience is not only physical. Each bodily sensation is associated with other experiences—emotional, social, intellectual, psychological, cultural, and sometimes financial. You can begin to explore your body in relation to your life story either chronologically, beginning with your first memory of your body, or in order of severity or importance.

Enumerating your own bodily changes

Begin by generating a list of all the bodily experiences and transformations you want to explore—your first shave, first menstrual period, your first sexual experience, your relationship to exercise, weight loss and gain, any accidents or episodes of sickness, including your recovery. Once you have created this list, think of the ways in which each experience affected you. You could even make a separate list for each item, exploring the other aspects of life that were affected by this transformation.

For example, how did your experience with weight loss affect the way you felt about yourself? Did you feel that others suddenly viewed you in a new light and treated you differently? Look at whether your relationships changed. Perhaps you bought a new wardrobe to complement the emergence of your new physical self. Did anything else about you change with your loss of weight? Did you become flirtatious, overconcerned about what you ate, obsessive about exercise? And how did you view your old self once you'd changed?

Explore your body like a map—its topography and landmasses, its treasures. See how time has left its mark and carved its lines. Listen to its movement like a whisper; hear when and where it collects your pleasures and pains.

The list can be extended as you analyze the subject. Exploring the other ways in which you were affected by this bodily change will help you depict the experience as whole, because one aspect of living always affects another and nothing is ever isolated or contained. Such transformations are always a fascinating topic, especially in relation to your life story.

You might want to include before-and-after photographs in your journal or scrapbook, or to document your entire transformation and particular bodily changes and experiences. For example, you could use tables or graphs to depict your physical training or to track your weight loss or gain. You might have kept ephemera from the hospital to highlight the experience of an accident, birth, recovery, or sickness, which could now be used to illustrate your story.

Note your emotional reactions to bodily changes.

For future reference, you might want to make notes of what it feels like to age. When did you first notice age-related changes in your body: Was it in your joints, the appearance of gray hair, menopause, or forgetfulness? Note your emotional reactions to these changes and how they affected your views on mortality. How did society's attitudes to aging affect your experience? Would the experience have been different if you had lived in another place or time?

Society, science, culture, technology, the government, and peers, all affect the personal relationships we have with our bodies, including what we choose to eat or wear, how often we visit the doctor or exercise, what measures we might take to prevent genetic ailments or disease, or how we might treat them.

As we age our relationships to our physical selves change. In relation to the external factors mentioned in the previous paragraph, how might you trace your development?

VOICES OF THE MASTERS

Jamaica Kincaid's memoir, *My Brother,* describes her brother Devon's battle against AIDS. A topic such as this can be a subject of your memoir, journal, or scrapbook. You could write about your body or the body of a loved one who has gone through a difficult time—whether because of cancer, AIDS, Alzheimer's, Parkinson's, drug addiction, or a tragic accident. Think about how this person changed as a result of his affliction, what your reaction was, and the effect on your relationship. Was there rehabilitation, and if so, what was your role? How did you change as you watched your loved one through this time; what did you learn about yourself?

When Kincaid's brother was dying of AIDS, she visited him in the hospital and supplied him with AZT, hoping to prolong his life. She also tried to understand the man he was, and reestablish their damaged relationship. In doing this with brutal self-reflection, she also learned a great deal about herself. In describing her brother's body, to convey his level of sickness, Kincaid writes:

When I first saw him in the hospital, lying there almost dead, his lips were scarlet red, as if layers and layers of skin had been removed and only one last layer remained, holding in place the dangerous fluid that was his blood.

The "layers" that she imagines removed hint at the layers of self she peeled back while writing the book. Writing about her brother's body ultimately meant writing about herself.

Weight loss is often a personal triumph; record your accomplishment alongside the emotional upheavals and struggles that you encountered on the way.

On Reading

In order to learn how to write, it's imperative that you read and, more important, learn to read like a writer. Writers not only read for pleasure but also take note of all things relevant to the craft of writing—plot and character development, sentence structure, choice of vocabulary, cadence, book or story structure, style, themes, pacing, voice, dialogue, and use of description. While all works of fiction employ these elements of craft, so do most memoirs. You should read both.

Analyze a piece of writing

Choose a short story or a section of a memoir and read it three or four times. Break it down sentence by sentence, noting the sentences' length and structure and the way the author develops characters or uses setting to advance the plot. Look at conflicts between characters, between characters and their environments or their goals; note how information was revealed and how tension was built. While reading like this requires effort, once you start realizing how a work is written, you can apply your observations to your own writing.

> **You may choose your reading based on what you want to write yourself.**

With so many memoirs on the market, you may not know where to begin. As discussed earlier, memoirs cover numerous topics or themes—coming of age, career, travel, adversity, relationships, and so on. You might choose your reading based on what you want to write yourself. The excerpts in this book introduce you to a variety of writers and may serve as a place to begin. Or you can visit your local bookstore or library and scan the shelf, selecting what appeals to you.

Opposite is a shortlist of recommended memoirs, grouped according to theme, some of which are sampled in this book. There are, of course, many more topics and titles to explore; use this list as a starting point.

When reading, consider how the author conveys her message, how she carefully selects every word and constructs every sentence and every paragraph so that the momentum of the story is constantly moving forward. Think of how she keeps the reader engaged, and if you find yourself drifting, make note of why. Keep a reading journal to record your reactions, observations, and thoughts, as well as any ideas that come to mind for your own life story.

To turn your pleasure reading into critical analysis is a difficult but important step. Take the time to observe how your favorite writers employ the relevant elements of craft, and apply what you learn to crafting your own life story.

WRITER'S WORKSHOP

Recommended memoirs include:

Coming of age

When I Was Puerto Rican, Esmeralda Santiago

Black Boy, Richard Wright

Out of Egypt, André Aciman

Running with Scissors, Augusten Burroughs

Bone Black, Memories of Girlhood, bell hooks

Speak Memory, Vladimir Nabokov

Coming of Age in Mississippi, Anne Moody

Stolen Lives, Twenty Years in a Desert Jail, Malika and Michelle Fitoussi

Woman Warrior: Memoirs of a Girlhood among Ghosts, Maxine Hong Kingston

An American Childhood, Annie Dillard

My Life in Orange, Tim Guest

I Know Why the Caged Bird Sings, Maya Angelou

An Open Book, Coming of Age in the Heartland, Michael Dirda

Bad Blood, Lorna Sage

Hoi Polloi, Craig Sherborn

The Road from Coorain, Jill Ker Conway

Travels by Night—a Memoir of the Sixties, George Fetherling

An Angel at My Table, Janet Frame

Over the Top With Jim, Hugh Lunn

Adversity

The Diary of a Young Girl, Anne Frank

Angela's Ashes, Frank McCourt

Jarhead: A Marine's Chronicle of the Gulf War and Other Battles, Arthur Swofford

An Evil Cradling, Brian Keenan

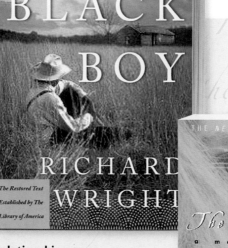

Relationships

The Kiss, Kathryn Harrison

Five Men Who Broke My Heart, Susan Shapiro

The Middle of Everything: Memoirs of Motherhood, Michelle Herman

Maus, Art Spiegelman

High Fidelity, Nick Hornby

Illness and dying

Signs of Life: A Memoir of Dying and Discovery, Tim Brooks

The Year of Magical Thinking, Joan Didion

Rowing Without Oars: A Memoir of Living and Dying, Ulla-Carin Lindquist

Girl, Interrupted, Susanna Kaysen

Borrowed Time: An AIDS Memoir, Paul Monette

The Diving Bell and the Butterfly: A Memoir of Life in Death, Jean-Dominique Bauby

Travel

In Patagonia, Bruce Chatwin

Area of Darkness, V. S. Naipaul

The Snow Leopard, Peter Matthiessen

Part Two

Organizing and Expressing Your Ideas

Staying Organized

Whether you choose to organize your collected data by date, subject, or theme, you must stay organized as you generate material for your life story. The first part of the book helped you consider what aspects of your life to write about and include in your life story. By now you should have a collection of lists, time lines, letters, photographs, ephemera, and even some writing samples. In this next part, we're going to look at how these ideas can be turned into stories for your journal, memoir, or scrapbook, but before we get started, it's important to address how to stay organized.

Keeping your material under control

If you've been keeping all of your material in a daily journal, then it will be organized by date. Unfortunately, unless the entry you're looking for is a write-up of a birthday party or a Thanksgiving meal, you may forget when something happened and have to search an entire book to find the material you need. Working on a computer, if you can, will make life easier, because no matter how much material you amass, you can use the various search facilities to help retrieve what you need almost instantly. Devote some time to devising a system that will work for you. It may not seem like a very creative task, but it will help you in the long run.

Whether you work with hard (printed out) or soft copy (directly on the computer) doesn't really matter—the same organization methods are required. You need to decide how to divide up and label your material in folders. You might choose to keep a separate folder for each collection of lists, time lines, first drafts, and so on, and label them as such. This way, when you're experiencing writer's block and looking for inspiration, you can open any folder and immediately access memories to inspire stories.

Organizing your material—the assembling of your facts, story snapshots, and ideas—benefits the development of your story structure.

Alternatively, you can arrange your material by subject, keeping it general, with labels such as "Relationships," "School," "Family," and "Travel." Or you might be more specific and label your folders with years, the names of your characters, phases in your life, or particular locations that have been significant to you, giving you folders that contain collections of lists, photographs, letters, and time lines. Whatever method you choose, you must be able to access the material without having to work your way through boxes or books or collections of loose pages. Nothing can delay you or deflate your inspiration more than not being able to access your data when you are ready to write.

Your subject matter will guide your folder labels. The more narrow your focus, the more specific the labels will be. For example, they could be as narrow as "Aunt Sonia's letters to her husband" or as general as "Story ideas—adventures with Sue, 1978–81."

> **You must be able to access the material without having to work your way through boxes or books.**

If you already have a clear idea of what your life-story project will be, along with a story line, then you can organize your material in the order in which you think the ingredients should appear (numbering each folder), while keeping the files separate in case you later need to restructure or rearrange your story. If you're uncertain about the structure at this stage, try making note cards for every chapter or anticipated scene, and pinning them up on a board (again, numbering the cards), where you can see them easily and move them around. You can then write the same number on each corresponding folder so you know where and when to access the material when it comes time to script each particular chapter or scene. Use this storyboard to guide you through your draft. Once you've generated pages, write the corresponding page numbers on the index cards so that if you later need to restructure your story, you can first rearrange the cards on the board and then cut and paste your sections or scenes until your life story has achieved a new order.

The same methods apply to your ephemera, letters, and photographs. Store your material in shoe boxes and accordion folders—and label them—unless you feel the material is precious and needs to be stored archivally. In this case, use acid-free paper and boxes, which will help preserve your material with no risk of contamination.

If working on a computer, always back up your material. Print hard copies, save material on disk, photocopy documents, and even copy as you go, if you are afraid of anything happening to the original. Writing your life story is a lot of work; you don't want to misplace or lose the material you have worked so hard to generate.

Making a Start

Moving on from the ideas stage might seem overwhelming, but it doesn't have to be, because you don't need to start at the beginning. Even if you are not entirely clear how you are going to structure your life story, you can begin by writing bits and pieces as they occur to you; this is less intimidating than attempting to write something from beginning to end. Once you have a collection of written pieces, you can add structure (see pages 128–131). But how do you even start writing bits and pieces?

Practicing discipline

One of the most important skills to develop when writing is discipline. The greatest amount of talent will get you nowhere if you don't have any discipline, but talent can be developed and nurtured with practice and patience. Try to write at the same time every day. Develop a schedule that allows you to write for a certain amount of time, say one hour before work, daily. Practice develops healthy habits.

> Thinking and reflecting are both part of the writing process.

Keep in mind that thinking and reflecting are both part of the writing process, especially when compiling a memoir, which involves a lot of time spent remembering. If you are having trouble starting and feel overwhelmed by the blank screen or page, refer back to your lists, time lines, and outlines, or to the exercises suggested or questions posed in the first part of this book. You might even use some of your other writings to inspire new ones. Does rereading a life-story excerpt or scene make you think of another experience that you haven't yet written about?

Decide upon a workspace and time that suits you. It could be writing on the commuter train, in a coffee shop, at the library, at your desk the same time every day, or in whatever quiet moments you can steal for yourself at home.

Writing a first draft

When you first attempt to write a vignette or an episode from your life, hold nothing back. Do not try to edit yourself while writing; do not worry if your story has good form. Simply begin, and keep writing until you can't write any more. When picking up where you left off the previous day, do not read the entirety of your previous day's script. Do not start editing or revising your first draft until the piece is done or you will get sidetracked. If you must, read only the last paragraph you wrote the day before and continue on. Only once you have reached the end should you look back.

If you already have a clear idea of where you want your life story to begin, try to start writing at that point. But keep in mind that you don't have to be married to where you start. The beginning of your story won't necessarily be the initial paragraph of your memoir. Sometimes you need to write a few paragraphs or pages, just to warm up. Maybe your story doesn't begin until page six, even though you started writing on page one--you may need to edit your work later to create a compelling beginning. We will return to this topic in Part Three (see pages 144–145) when it comes time to revise.

Whether you're producing a journal, memoir, or scrapbook, you will eventually need to produce a complete first draft. With a scrapbook this may mean simply listing the experiences or times you want to document and creating an outline that suggests a layout. The first draft of a journal or memoir is likely to take more time. Either way, putting words on paper (or computer screen) is a critical step toward creating your life story.

The reason it's called a first draft is because it's meant to be revisited and revised. If you feel that

you're going off on a tangent when scripting your first draft, don't cut yourself short; go with it. This may eventually become another chapter, short story, or book.

The beginning of your story is what will draw the reader in and make her want to read on. Keep in mind that the beginning of every chapter should be compelling. What is it that makes a memoir reader want to read on? Suspense, action, an active protagonist, and a certain level of self-awareness. Beginning with a scene that incorporates these elements is more likely to get your readers' attention than a proclamation or a rumination.

Your ideas and inspirations may come in waves. Be sure that you capture whatever thoughts, ideas, or memories come to mind. Even if some of your efforts are fleeting, they're all building blocks that will ultimately benefit your story's construction.

> The beginning of your story is what will draw the reader in.

Writing Clearly

Grammar and punctuation are your essential tools. If you're unsure of the rules behind language use, you risk confusing the reader. Your writing will also suffer stylistically: how you shape your language—choosing short, sharp sentences rather than a long, meandering passage, for example—communicates as much to your audience as the words themselves.

Refining your prose

New writers frequently mix verb tenses, fluctuating between past and present. When reading your drafts, make sure your tenses are consistent—either all past or all present—unless the switch is a deliberate style device. The same goes for point of view. If you begin your story in the first person (using "I"), don't suddenly start referring to yourself as "he" or "she."

Mistakes can often be detected by reading your work aloud. Listen hard for sentences that are too wordy or poorly constructed. If you can reduce four words to one, do it. Consider the economic language of poetry and try to mimic this. (Read poetry and note the absence of excess words.) Do not try to show off by constructing long, elaborate sentences; they will only confuse the reader and make her lose interest. Avoid using too many adjectives and adverbs in descriptions. Keep your language as concrete as possible (grounded in verbs and nouns). If you are in any doubt regarding grammar and usage, consult one of the respected guides that are widely available, such as Strunk and White's *The Elements of Style*.

Respecting the rules of language use doesn't have to mean cramping your style inside a straitjacket of standard English, but flair counts for nothing if you don't say what you mean. Keep your readers interested by using language that is clear and precise.

Pay close attention to your word choice. Be careful not to begin every sentence with "I" or "The." Vary your openers with a mix of articles, nouns, verbs, pronouns, and proper nouns. Also be aware of words repeating within the same paragraph. While the reader may not notice the repetition of the word "said," she will make note of your employing the adjective "cautious" repeatedly. If you are having problems finding alternative words, consult a thesaurus.

You should also seek to vary your sentence length and structure. Break up a series of long sentences with one or two that are short. This helps to keep the reader engaged and gives her room to breathe. Do not introduce each character with a paragraph dedicated to his or her appearance; reveal that information as it becomes necessary. And be careful not to begin each scene with your character's entrance into the room.

> Remember that your job as a writer is to communicate clearly.

Although sentence structure can be aided by reading your work aloud, paragraph structure requires a closer look. A paragraph should contain sentences that support or are related to a single idea. A new paragraph begins when a thought is complete or when a new idea, thought, or speaker is introduced. Every time a new speaker takes over, skip to the next line and indent to indicate a fresh paragraph.

It takes time to establish a voice—the character or feel of the narration, or the essence or presence behind what links the words together—and you should be aware of the difference between a speaking voice and the voice on the page. Write as you speak only when this is your intent. If your

narrator is not supposed to narrate the story with your speaking voice (which should generally be the case), then save your speaking voice for the dialogue that falls between quotation marks.

Remember that your job as a writer is to communicate clearly, to minimize the possibility of confusing your reader, and to keep tenses, dates, and facts consistent (if someone has dark hair in one chapter, make sure he isn't blond in another). Practice and patience lead to perfection. If you read and write with awareness, you will develop the skills to get your story across to the reader with the exact meaning you intend.

One of the tricky things about writing a memoir is the difference between protagonist and narrator, who are often the same person: you. Keep in mind that your protagonist is aware only of his or her present situation and past, while the narrator is all-knowing. If you find a shift in voice when rereading your life story, it might be because the narrator has suddenly taken over by telling the reader the story of the protagonist's thoughts, feelings, or plight. Use the narrator's knowledge to structure and craft your story, but do not let his or her voice dominate the revealing of your protagonist's life. Let the reader see your protagonist live.

Use a thesaurus to avoid careless word repetitions and, if you're unsure of how a word is used, take the time to look it up in a dictionary.

Audience: Writing for Yourself

When writing for yourself, your approach and structure depend largely upon your subject and your goals. Assuming you want to do more than keep a standard journal—generally a series of entries written about experiences immediately after they occur—you need to consider both what you want to focus on and how you want to present these aspects of your life story in your writing.

Defining your goals

You may decide to create a private scrapbook, featuring photographs and images that have personal resonance. Alternatively, you may want to redraft an existing journal, expanding upon and changing what you wrote immediately after the events had occurred.

> Perhaps you want to create a complete or partial self-portrait.

Either way, you need to define your goals. Do you want to acquire a better understanding of a particular relationship, situation, or experience, or do you want to resolve or overcome a certain struggle or dilemma? Do you want to document your most private transitions during a difficult time? Or do you want to embark on a journey, either with another person or in search of someone or something, hoping to gain a deeper awareness through your writing? Maybe you are undergoing therapy or some kind of recovery and you want to write about your revelations and struggles in order to better understand yourself. Or perhaps you want to create a complete or partial self-portrait—your journal being a representation of you during a significant chapter in your life.

If you kept a diary throughout the specific time period you happen to be writing about, use it as your memory (for all those long-forgotten details), your map, or even your first draft.

VOICES OF THE MASTERS

Frida Kahlo's diary is an illustrated journal that documents the Mexican artist's thoughts and dreams, her relationship with one of Mexico's greatest muralists, Diego Rivera, her polio, and the suffering she endured as a result of the streetcar accident that broke her spinal column, collarbone, ribs, and pelvis, and fractured her polio-stricken leg.

In the following excerpt, from 1950–51, we get a glimpse of her road to recovery and of what it was that kept her alive. Although we don't know if she wrote exclusively for herself or if she hoped for publication, it is clear that her work (including the writing of this journal) bolstered her will to survive.

A critic once wrote of Frida Kahlo that her paintings, which consisted mostly of self-portraits, were her biography. In a similar way, feel free to express yourself in any medium you like when creating your own journal.

I've been sick for a year now. Seven operations on my spinal column. Doctor Farill saved me. He brought me back the joy of life. I am still in the wheelchair, and I don't know if I'll be able to walk again soon. I have a plaster corset [and] even though it is a frightful nuisance, it helps my spine. I don't feel any pain. Only this…bloody tiredness, and naturally, quite often, despair. A despair which no words can describe. I'm still eager to live. I've started to paint again. A little picture to give to Dr. Farill on which I'm working with all my love. I feel uneasy about my painting. Above all I want to transform it into something useful for the Communist revolutionary movement, since up to now I have only painted the earnest portrayal of myself, but I'm very far from work that could serve the Party. I have to fight with all my strength to contribute the few positive things my health allows me to the revolution. The only true reason to live for.

Kahlo used her journal to record memories and document her thoughts, experiences, and feelings. Comprised of text interspersed with and set alongside her paintings and drawings, many of which are self-portraits (see pages 96–97), the journal provides the reader with a sense of Frida Kahlo—the artist, the lover, the patient, the revolutionary—in her entirety.

The beauty of writing solely for yourself is the freedom it ensures. However, it is still important to challenge yourself—to find the right words, to express yourself clearly, and to employ the appropriate structure that best suits your story, whether this is a series of vignettes, journal-like entries, letters, poems, essays, or something more visual with supporting text.

If you have trouble accessing the deeper regions of your emotional pool, your fantasies, or your memories, you might try treating yourself as a character by writing about yourself in the third person, using "she" or "he." Because your audience is limited to you, you have fewer rules to follow. What you should prioritize is identifying your goals and reaching them by whatever means necessary. You've made the decision to begin your life-story project for a reason, and most likely it will be the journey traveled that ends up mattering far more than the end product.

Audience: Writing for Family and Friends

If you've decided to create a scrapbook for family and friends, then chances are you generally know what your project will contain. A scrapbook is similar to a photo album but differs from it in that it uses text and aims to tell a story. Think about how much of your story you want to tell. How narrow is the focus of your story? Do you intend to document your entire life or your family's history, including the lives of your ancestors, or do you want to explore only a slice of your life? Is your scrapbook someone else's biography—does it cover your parents, children, or a loved one who has passed away?

Singling out your story and your audience

Think of the message you want to convey or the story you want to tell and decide who you are producing this story for. Are you documenting your family history for future generations? Using the scrapbook to share your travels or recipes? Making a gift for a fiftieth wedding anniversary? Hoping to heal the loss of a loved one by documenting your lives together? Helping your children recall the childhood they might forget?

Since you might not yet be sure just how much information you want to include in your scrapbook, you should begin by looking through your material. Do you have a large collection of photographs or memorabilia? If you don't have much of either, you can illustrate your text with drawings, paintings, and objects. Look through your material and separate your images or ephemera by dates, people, occasions, or themes, while keeping in mind that you'll need to be selective later on when deciding what to include. If seeing an image brings a story to mind, jot it down so you can reference it later. If you find your collection isn't as complete as you'd like, make a list of the images you will need to fill in the gaps—either by taking new photographs, borrowing pictures from family and friends, or by finding images elsewhere. The process of selecting the visuals from your collection should give you ideas for a story line or help you firm up a story you have in mind.

Just as photographs from the past serve to trigger your memories and to fill in the gaps, think of how you might serve the children you know by capturing the early segments of their lives—the many firsts they experience and their initial displays of personality.

Relating the story behind the pictures

Before you consider how you are going to illustrate your scrapbook, decide how you intend to include text. Do you want to limit your words to captions or do you plan to include journal-like entries, letters, or stories? Once you have decided how much you want to write, think about how you want to employ your words. You may want to use text to connect the spaces between your pieces of memorabilia in order to tell the story behind the pictures, capture how you felt at the moment of the event, or address your audience. Identifying your audience, your story, and your message will help you decide how best to employ text.

Your photographs and memorabilia might provide a good basis for your life story, but you can take your scrapbook to another level by allotting equal emphasis to images and text. Think how rich and developed your final product will be if you include text that isn't necessarily inspired by the images but that shows another side of the story— possibly a surprising or personal one. Perhaps your story charts your battle against a serious illness, in which case you might interrupt the main narrative with pieces on your hopes and dreams for your family should you pass away. Another way of adding depth to a story is through comparison: you could compare and contrast old memories of your childhood with those that are now unfolding.

If you want your life story to be a visual display, then you might choose to emphasize the times in your life for which you have a lot of memorabilia and souvenirs—an excursion, a collecting phase, or a time when you were most culturally active and engaged.

Audience: Writing for Publication

The act of writing for publication differs greatly from writing for yourself, family, or friends. Right from the beginning, you must pay closer attention to story and character development, structure, themes, pacing, and description. You'll generally need to rely less on image and more heavily on words to tell your story; it is how you choose to organize these words that will determine your story's success.

Developing your theme

As a memoir writer, you need to determine what deserves to be told and in which order you should arrange your material. A fascinating life doesn't necessarily make a great book. If a writer doesn't have a presence on the page, can't identify his life's themes, or doesn't know which observations or experiences to exclude, then chances are that his story won't be worth reading. But if you can bring your characters to life, create tension and drama, master dialogue, and develop themes, then even the most ordinary life or seemingly mundane experiences can be developed into a great memoir.

A memoir doesn't span your entire life chronologically. It isolates a specific time, passage, relationship, setting, experience, or theme and usually employs flashbacks and flash forwards as a way to manipulate time and control pacing.

As the first part of this book discussed, deciding on your theme, or themes, is important. Stories written for a public audience should revolve around a theme with universal appeal, such as the need to love and be loved, ambition, loneliness and isolation, or rejection. Within this big picture, you need to have a particular approach, idea, or experience that makes the story uniquely yours, something that separates you from the rest of humanity, whether it's your use of description, your

Before submitting your work for publication, ensure that it is edited and revised until it seems nothing more can change. Follow the publisher's protocol and requests, and always make your presentation professional and neat.

experience, or your interpretation of a situation. This is what will make your story linger in the reader's mind long after it's been read. If you have already decided on a central theme—your travels or career, for example—you might be surprised to find sub-themes emerging (see page 122). Identifying these sub-themes will help determine how you should structure your memoir.

> How you choose to organize your words will determine your story's success.

You may want to tell two completely different stories, but bring them together because they took place over the same time period to members of the same family: maybe dad was left at home to make a treehouse while the rest of the family went camping for the weekend; the final pages could see the family reunited, admiring the garden's new addition.

If the exercises and suggestions in Part One didn't guide you toward a theme, try writing until your story and its themes emerge naturally. As unorganized as it sounds, sometimes the only way to find a theme is to amass a collection of writings and let what you have written steer you toward a cohesive story and structure.

Themes will naturally emerge as you explore the life you've lived. It's up to you to recognize them once they're committed to the page.

VOICES OF THE MASTERS

Tobias Wolf explores his experience growing up in the 1950s in his book, *This Boy's Life*. In the opening paragraph he draws the reader in with an action scene and quickly introduces the book's central themes: his relationship with his mother, being on the lam, and living a life out of control. In just one short paragraph, the reader already has a picture of the writer's childhood.

Our car boiled over again just after my mother and I crossed the Continental Divide. While we were waiting for it to cool we heard, from somewhere above us, the bawling of an airhorn. The sound got louder and then a big truck came around the corner and shot past us into the next curve, its trailer shimmying wildly. We started after it. "Oh Toby," my mother said, "he's lost his brakes."

The Self-portrait

The self-portrait—a visual representation of oneself, whether symbolic, representative, or idealized—is a classic part of the artist's repertoire and may have a useful place in your life story. Producing a self-portrait—through a photograph, painting, or collage of bits and pieces that represent you—may help you express what you have trouble saying with words and allow you more freedom of expression.

Artists' self-portraits

Frida Kahlo (see pages 90–91) began painting after a horrific streetcar accident left her bedridden. With a mirror over her bed, she painted a series of self-portraits, which became her autobiography.

> Studying the self-portraits of artists you admire may give you inspiration to produce your own.

Frida Kahlo's *Self-Portrait with Cropped Hair* depicts the artist seated in a man's suit holding the pair of scissors she'd used to sever the strands of hair that are now scattered around her on the floor. The caption above her in the portrait reads, "If I used to love you, it was because of your hair, now that you are bald, I don't love you any more." Painted in 1940, at a time when her health was deteriorating once again, the image of despair was painted in response to her divorce from Diego Rivera. On more than one of the occasions on which she'd found Rivera with another woman, she cut off the long locks that he loved. This image of herself is far removed from her more typical depictions that show the artist in traditional Mexican dresses with long flowing hair, thereby emphasizing her despair.

Studying the self-portraits of artists you admire may give you inspiration to produce your own. Remember, however, that self-portraits are often very revealing both psychologically and physically. Once you have produced a portrait, and released it to others, you cannot control how others respond.

Self-portraits are a great opportunity to explore and reveal various aspects of your personality and moods. Try to make your portrait—be it a painting or photograph— as candid as possible.

VOICES OF THE MASTERS

Lucy Grealy, whose *Autobiography of a Face* recounts her experience of cancer, takes time out of the narrative to describe herself in the passage below. You may feel that a written self-portrait would be more appropriate in your life story.

My pleasure at the sight of the children didn't last long, however. I knew what was coming. As soon as they got over the thrill of being near the ponies, they'd notice me. Half my jaw was missing, which gave my face a strange triangular shape, accentuated by the fact that I was unable to keep my mouth completely closed. When I first started doing pony parties, my hair was still short and wispy, still growing in from the chemo. But as it grew I made things worse by continuously bowing my head and hiding behind the curtain of hair, furtively peering out at the world like some nervous actor. Unlike the actor, though, I didn't secretly relish my audience, and if it were possible I would have stood behind that curtain forever, my head bent in an eternal act of deference. I was, however, dependent upon my audience. Their approval or disapproval defined everything for me, and I believed with every cell in my body that approval wasn't written into my particular script. I was fourteen years old.

Lucy Grealy's Autobiography of a Face *recounts her traumatic experience of cancer of the jaw. It also charts the emotional journey she took in battling this disease.*

Brian Keenan, in *An Evil Cradling*, uses a description of his changed physical appearance to reflect the traumatic experience he had as a hostage in Beirut:

I looked for a moment at my reflection in the convex curve of the spoon and was frozen with shock.... Black pools under my eyes, my hair long and askew like a wet mop that had been left to dry in the sun. My beard was longer than I had known it ever to be. My body from the neck down seemed so frail in that curvature, like the body of someone with serious malnutrition. I looked tiny and bony and my face sat huge upon my shoulders, out of proportion, not part of this body.

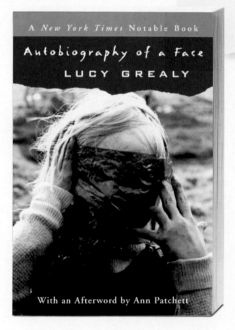

A *New York Times* Notable Book

Autobiography of a Face

LUCY GREALY

With an Afterword by Ann Patchett

Exploring the Self in Poetry

Because the self is a prominent theme in poetry, you might want to include some poems in your journal or scrapbook. Even if you have no desire to make poetry a part of your life story, try writing some poems—they may help you remember and reflect.

Try your hand at poetry. This list of exercises will help get you started writing poems. It should assist you in concentrating your language to express the essence of a feeling or experience. Keep in mind that a poem doesn't have to be as long as a story or a book and can be either literal or abstract. It is usually arranged in lines, in metrical or rhythmic form, but doesn't have to rhyme if you don't want it to. Poetry often uses richer, more concentrated language than prose. If you like your poem, you can incorporate it into your life story or take what you learn from it and develop it into a story or scene.

The box shows just a few suggestions; the possibilities for poem themes are endless. Try incorporating poetry into your life story, or take what you discovered in a poem and develop it into a story.

WRITERS WORKSHOP

- **DIALOGUE POEM**: Capture a conversation like a snapshot, either one you've overheard or your own.

- **COLLAGE POEM**: Clip text from newspapers and magazines, then cut and paste the words to form a poem.

- **DREAM POEM**: Use poetry to recall, imagine, or interpret a dream.

- **FEELINGS POEM**: Write a poem describing a feeling, without naming the feeling itself.

- **HAIKU**: Reflect on a memory in three lines, using only 5 syllables in the first, 7 in the second, and 5 in the last.

- **LETTER POEM**: Liberate your feelings toward someone by writing a letter in poetry, which you know you won't send.

- **LIST POEM**: Use the lists suggested in this book to create a poem.

- **ODE**: Honor who or what is important to you.

- **PLACE POEM**: Use poetry to describe your neighborhood, your bedroom, your favorite place in the world, or somewhere you go to find peace.

- **PHOTOGRAPH POEM**: Write about a photograph or about the memory it inspires.

but close

as a door slams

ALMOST SIXTY:

from now on

even begonias

are amazing

You can use poetry to explore the economy of language. Observe how poets minimize their word use when communicating moods, scenes, moments, feelings, and thoughts.

Jim Moore, the author of six collections of poetry, published the following poem in the *New Yorker*. A remembrance of a few events that culminates with a celebration of his nearly sixty years, Moore's "Invisible Strings" is an intimate portrait that encapsulates not just relationships, but loneliness as well.

Seven Invisible Strings

1

I remember my mother toward the end,

    folding the tablecloth after dinner
      so carefully,
    as if it were the flag
      of a country that no longer existed,
    but once had ruled the world.

2

Almost 8 A.M., curtain drawn shut, lying in bed, naked:

    it's not the same as sex,
    but close,
      as a door slams,
    a shoe crunches on gravel,
      walking away.
    Then the long afterward of lying still—
      happy, lonely,
    who can say which—
      the world
    just as it is, and the lover, too
      just so.

3

This spring night,

    everyone at the party
younger than me
    except for one man.
We give each other the secret password.

4

On this cloudy May day,

    I keep thinking
    maybe June is what I need
      to make me happy.

5

Tears? Of course, but also the marsh grass

    near the Mississippi:
    your whispers and mine,
      and the dog's long contented sighs.

6

Helicopter flies overhead

    reminding me of that old war
      where one friend lost his life,
    one his mind
      and one came back happy
    to be missing only an unnecessary finger.

7

Almost sixty:

    from now on
      even begonias are amazing.

Happiness and contentment are so near they seem tangible, despite the dinner's end, the lover's departure, age, cloudy days, and war. In the final stanza, the poet swears to enjoy life to the fullest—a lesson it took nearly 60 years to learn.

Memoir and Fiction

Just like fiction, a memoir must be developed with close attention to character and plot development and themes. Both genres make use of dialogue, description, point of view, voice, setting, and pacing. Although the author of a memoir already knows the plot of her story, like the fiction writer, she must decide how best to arrange her material and determine what to leave out.

The memoir as a story

As in fiction, the protagonist of a memoir must be searching for something—she must have something at stake. This requires the memoir writer to present her life as a story, with a beginning, middle, and end. In addition, your responsibility is the same as the fiction writer's—to build suspense and tension, to keep the reader engaged through the story's momentum, and to introduce universal themes while shedding new light on a familiar situation, character, struggle, or story.

VOICES OF THE MASTERS

Italo Calvino, an Italian writer of world renown, begins his short story, "The Adventure of a Soldier," with the paragraph below. The excerpt is taken from Calvino's collection of stories, *Difficult Loves:*

In the compartment, a lady came and sat down, tall and buxom, next to Private Tomagra. She must have been a widow from the provinces, to judge by her dress and her veil: the dress was black silk, appropriate for prolonged mourning, but with useless frills and furbelows; and the veil went all around her face falling from the brim of a massive, old-fashioned hat. Other places were free, there in the compartment, Private Tomagra noticed, and he had assumed the widow would surely choose one of them. But, on the contrary, despite the vicinity of a coarse soldier like himself, she came and sat right there—no doubt for some reason connected with travel, the soldier quickly decided, a draft, or the direction of the train.

Like Calvino, you can reveal your own or another's character through writing with close attention to inner thoughts.

Including obstacles

If your life experiences are less action-packed than most novels, perhaps your plot might revolve around an internal struggle or a more personal or private plight. Just because you haven't traveled around the world, saved endangered species, or run a nation aground doesn't mean you can't create tension in your text. Once you identify what is at stake for your protagonist, you can create tension by including obstacles and antagonists.

Your story doesn't have to be full of wildly dramatic events for it to be interesting. It's the way you create tension, even in everyday matters— such as the first date with a potential partner, for example—that makes the story engrossing.

Vivian Gornick's nonfiction essay "On Living Alone," from her collection *Approaching Eye Level*, makes an interesting contrast.

> *It's Sunday morning, and I'm walking up Columbus Avenue. Couples are coming at me on all sides. They fill the street from building line to pavement edge. Some are clasped together looking raptly into each other's faces, some are holding hands, their eyes restless, window-shopping; some walk by side by side, stony-faced, carefully not touching. I have the sudden conviction that half these people will, in a few months, be walking with someone else now walking on the avenue one half of another couple. Eventually that arrangement will terminate as well, and each man and each woman will once again be staring out the window of a room empty of companionship. This is a population in a permanent state of intermittent attachment. Inevitably, the silent apartment lies in wait.*

Although she doesn't come out and say it, the narrator clearly longs for some kind of companionship. The search for understanding what she senses as her predicament—a life alone—is what the reader understands to be her quest.

Although the first passage is fiction and the second nonfiction, written in the third and first person, respectively, both writers employ similar techniques. In each of these opening paragraphs, we are introduced to the story's protagonist (narrator), are given a setting, and get a sense of the kind of journey the protagonist is about to begin: the soldier is about to embark on some kind of relationship with the widow, while Gornick, who longs not to be lonely, will attempt to remedy her predicament.

Character

The main character in a story is the protagonist, and in a memoir the protagonist is usually the writer, who is scripting his life story—but they are not one and the same thing. Though initially confusing, it is important to identify the differences between the protagonist, who is experiencing the story as it happens, and the author/narrator, who has already experienced all that is being told. The narrator possesses knowledge of the story's beginning, middle, and end, but the protagonist cannot be aware of an event before it actually happens.

Charting the protagonist's journey

When writing a memoir, the author shapes the character's experience on the page by allowing time to pass (using flashbacks and flash forwards when necessary). Time allows the writer to view his experience in retrospect and allows him to gain distance from the individual he was when the life experience occurred. This helps him become the author who knows his protagonist inside and out.

Just as in fiction, the protagonist is meant to lead the reader on a journey. The protagonist must have an objective, must want something, and should come across antagonists and obstacles along the way; these difficulties are what make a story interesting. Imagine how dull a story would be if the protagonist immediately achieved all his goals. The antagonist can reside outside of the protagonist and take the form of a person, society, religion, nature, political view, or the character's own past. The resistance can also come from within—a struggle within the protagonist's mind (you can include both if you want). While the protagonist may initially be unaware of these obstacles or people in her path, or be unable to identify them at the moment, the narrator knows them well.

Try to show what the protagonist thinks and feels by showing her gestures and expressions, her choices, body language, interactions, and how she speaks.

What is it that your protagonist seeks? Will she achieve her goals and change, will she fail but still grow, or will she remain completely unchanged? What will be her relationship with her antagonist(s)? All of these elements come together to create the plot, which is a result of the protagonist's actions. Just as with obstacles or antagonists, these actions can be internal or external.

Be selective when revealing your characters' traits to your reader. Restrict yourself to description that is relevant to the story. The reader must not be allowed to know everything about your characters, including yourself; too many facts will overwhelm and bore him. Think of your protagonist's journey and how it moves forward, and give only information that contributes to the story's momentum. If some detail about one of your characters doesn't contribute to the overall story, eliminate it.

If you have made lists for each of your main characters, now is the time to put them to use. When considering a character's physical appearance, for example, you should note looks, dress, gestures, and the person's physical presence—how he fills a room (or not) or interacts with others. His history will offer a sense of how he became the individual he is today—his family, politics, religion, education, friends, romantic relationships, occupation, income, and so on. His personality will reveal things like his best qualities and worst faults, his biggest fears, his hobbies, his deepest secret, his habits, expectations, favorites, loves, and hates.

How can you go about revealing your character's traits once you've decided what's relevant? You can

> How you choose to organize your words will determine your story's success.

make use of description, dialogue, action, and reporting the thoughts of your character. An unconscious reaction to a situation will often reveal more about the character than what he actually says. Be careful not to overburden the reader with a complete description—let it seep out gradually.

Just as conflict makes a story interesting, it also helps develop character. What are your character's

When writing about individuals you've never met, look for hints of character in letters, diaries, and photographs, in interviews and lifestyles.

conflicts; what are her faults? All characters have faults, but the narrator should never appear to judge. Judgment creates two-dimensional characters; it renders them flat. Present the facts and let the reader make up her own mind.

How a character acts with and for others is often different than how she behaves on her own. Does this split in her personality cause any conflict in your protagonist's life?

Character—the Portrait

Most of us have taken snapshots of family and friends, but how many of these pictures have in any way captured the essence of the person being photographed? In your scrapbook you may want to include pictures of your child smiling as she blows out the candles on her birthday cake, but you should also make an attempt to create images that give the viewer a sense of your subject's inner being or hidden traits—what she unknowingly reveals in her inner, unspoken reactions to an encounter or situation.

Capturing the inner self

In what ways can you reveal the subject's inner self? You might try capturing her off-guard, avoiding the posed picture altogether. Whether your sitter is in mid conversation, mid-stride, or mid-thought, you may well be able to catch her without her mask.

Look at this photograph by Dorthea Lange entitled "Migrant Mother" that was taken for the Farm Security Administration, a project meant to document the plight of U.S. migrant farm workers during the Great Depression. Photographed with three of her children, who hide from the camera as they seek comfort and safety in their mother, the subject, Florence Thompson, is full of despair. The clothes, the conditions of the sitters, and their body language, all depict a life of struggle. Thompson's furrowed brow and the pressure of her fingers that dig into the side of her face are details that contribute to this portrait of a woman with more pressing issues on her mind, than the present moment with the photographer.

When taking someone's portrait, consider not just the sitter, her expression, position, and dress, but also the light, foreground, and backdrop. What does the relationship between the sitter and her environment suggest about her character?

To capture a person's essence, a photographer need not always take her sitter by surprise. (The same can be applied to painted or drawn portraits.) Many photographers and artists posed their subjects. Take, for example, the photograph shown on the right by Gertrude Kasebier, a photographer well known for her portraits of women and children. In plate 79, "Portrait (Miss N)," Kasebier captures her subject, a young beauty, as a temptress. Leaning forward into the camera, with a direct sultry stare and bare soldiers, Miss N grips a pitcher in her hand. The sitter and her vessel present a portrait of a young woman, ripe and sexy.

> To capture a person's essence, a photographer need not always take her sitter by surprise.

When attempting to capture your sitter (whether the photograph is posed or not), be mindful of her body language, attire, and facial expression. Consider the objects in the frame as you would information in a paragraph. Are they relevant? If not, edit them out. Look at your subject's surroundings: Is he at ease in his setting or unsure? Assess the composition: How much of the frame does he fill? This should help reveal what you as the photographer see in your subject, alongside what you are or aren't willing to expose.

Beyond photography

In portraiture, you don't need to limit yourself to photographs. As with self-portraits, your images can be actual or representative, symbolizing what you think of your subject or how your subject chooses to represent herself. The mask the person

chooses to wear can be just as interesting as what lies beneath. Besides photographs, paintings, and drawings, you can also use collage to represent your character. Whatever your medium, try to capture your subject in a manner that might surprise her; the way in which you pose your subject might even suggest something about you or your relationship. Even if you don't plan to include this type of imagery in your life story, portraiture is still worthy of being explored. Just like writing poetry, you never know what you'll find. A visual exploration might be just what it takes to capture what you cannot put into words.

The photographer's relationship with her subject will determine how much the sitter is willing to expose, since it's the photographer's responsibility to create whatever mood or effect she hopes to achieve— tension or tranquillity.

Dialogue

There's no better way to display the characters of your life story than in a scene. A scene consists of dialogue and stage directions (the way in which characters occupy the setting) and is generally the only opportunity the reader gets to observe characters in present time. Though most memoirs are written in the past tense, dialogue is tied to the moment when it is spoken and a scene unfolds in the present, allowing the reader to "witness" the event as it occurs, rather than learn of it through the narrator as she recalls or interprets it later.

Giving voice to your characters

Since your characters are real-life individuals with whom you've spent a significant amount of time, you should have a sense of how they speak—word choice, tone, and diction—and of how they occupy the stage—with body language, gestures, pauses, and their interpretation of personal space. Not only is it important to capture your characters' speech, you also need to convey the truth behind what isn't or can't be said—the subtext—whether it's with silence, a nervous tic, a glance, rapid speech, by changing the subject, or with lies that the reader recognizes, or comes to recognize, as such.

Dialogue belongs in quotation marks, unless you choose not to use them at all, as Frank McCourt did in his memoir, *Angela's Ashes* (see opposite). This can be an effective means of indicating to your reader that your dialogue isn't wholly accurate.

Effective use of dialogue

Think of your dialogue as precious goods, and remember that not all spoken words belong on the page. If the dialogue doesn't further the momentum of the story or plot, don't include it. For example, if one of your characters picks up the phone, we do not need to hear, "Hi, how are you? I'm fine,"

unless it contributes something to character development or plot. You can better convey what you need to by indirect dialogue: I told him what he had done to me and Diane confirmed it. Or by relaying communication through exposition: I told him I couldn't go because I had to meet my sister.

Your character's presence in a scene can be revealed through dialogue, tone of voice, how she occupies her space on the stage, and what she chooses to withhold.

Characters are often identified with tags—he said, she screamed—but you should ensure that your characters sound unique: that their voices are individual enough to be recognized without having to identify each speaker on every line. Remember, too, that while the tag "said" can be used regularly, other tags, such as "screamed" or "whispered," do not bear such frequent repetition. It's also worth noting that people don't laugh or smile words. If a character in your story smiles, start a new sentence: "I love you." She smiled.

> Be sure that your dialogue is tight, that your speakers convey their meaning as quickly as possible.

While it's crucial that you mimic real-life dialogue as best you can, it's important to make sure that you do not allow your characters to go on and on, as speakers often do in real life. Be sure that your dialogue is tight, that your speakers convey their meaning as quickly as possible (unless they are rambling for a reason, like having something to hide). Use contractions, as speakers do, and try to keep your speakers' lines brief—back and forth—unless a particular character is prone to long monologues, and even then you'll want to break up the block of text on the page by having another character interject with a nod of the head or with a phrase such as "I see."

When you've finally created a scene, read your dialogue aloud; see if it captures each speaker's individual voice. Review the scene to ensure that the story's momentum maintains a reasonable pace; make sure each speaker reveals something new with each gesture or speech. Above all, be aware of your reader's time, which is valuable and should never be wasted with carelessly scripted scenes.

VOICES OF THE MASTERS

Frank McCourt uses minimal stage direction and description to draw portraits of his mother and father in the following scene from *Angela's Ashes*. His dialogue is carefully selected to develop tension and to inform the reader of what's at stake—his parents' relationship, the family's survival, and, in his father's eyes, the state of Ireland.

He comes to the bedroom door. Up, boys, up. A nickel for everyone who promises to die for Ireland….

Up, boys, up. Francis, Malachy, Oliver, Eugene. The Red Branch Knights, the Fenian Men, the IRA. Up, up.

Mam is at the kitchen table, shaking, her hair hanging damp, her face wet. Can't you leave them alone? she says. Jesus, Mary, and Joseph, isn't it enough that you come home without a penny in your pocket without making fools of the children on top of it?

She comes to us. Go back to bed, she says.

I want them up, he says. I want them ready for the day Ireland will be free from the center of the sea.

Don't cross me, she says, for if you do it'll be a sorry day in your mother's house.

He pulls his cap down over his face and cries, My poor mother. Poor Ireland. Och, what are we going to do?

Mam says, You're pure stone mad, and she tells us again to go to bed.

Plot

Whatever kind of story you are writing, it must have a plot—a structure upon which you can hang your life story and that will give your narrative shape. In this case, the plot will be based on events from your life: your actions, the results or consequences of your actions, your response to external situations, or your internal perspective. It is this chain of cause and effect that gives your reader something to follow.

Your protagonist's objective

Even if your memoir is not an action-packed adventure, you will have to decide upon a course of action for your protagonist to follow. Her course of action will be determined by her goals—what is it that your protagonist is after? What does she seek? Is her goal to overcome an illness, to get out of her small town, to travel across Russia in search of her heritage, to become the first female in her law firm, to understand her relationship with her mother, or to come to terms with her sexuality? Once you identify your protagonist's objective, you can determine the time period over which your story spans, whether it's 24 hours or half a century. With this chunk of time in mind, you can begin to consider your beginning, middle, and end.

Identifying your protagonist's objective will also enable you to determine what aspects of your life to include and what to leave out. For example, if you are writing about how you came to be a musician, you should only include the characters who influenced, directed, or distracted you in relation to this goal, alongside the experiences that led you there. The reader needn't spend much time with the neighbor you developed a crush on, nor get as frustrated as you did enduring the many hours you spent working in a coffee shop. All aspects of the story should help illuminate the pathway of your protagonist's journey to ensure your reader a feeling of closure when all the strands of the story are pulled together at the end.

The context of your protagonist's plight, the time period and culture in which he lives, will reveal something of his person, what he has to work with or against; use this information to help develop your plot.

Arriving at the port

Bon Voyage!

On board, leaving New York

Classic plot structure

The classic story structure—beginning, middle, and end—isn't the only way in which to shape a plot, but your protagonist has to begin at one place and end up at another, even if you choose to begin your story at the end. It is essential that your protagonist experience some kind of evolution. The change might be that the protagonist comes to accept herself and her relationship with her mother, as in Vivian Gornick's *Fierce Attachments*. In Susan Kaysen's *Girl Interrupted*, a memoir that covers the author's two years in a psychiatric hospital, the change is charted over a specific period of time, from her admission at the story's beginning to her release at its end.

> You should use your beginning to introduce your main characters.

If you choose to employ the classic story structure, you should use your beginning to introduce your main characters, their setting, and the situation. Since you want to draw your reader in as quickly as possible, you might also choose to begin your story with some kind of action, something that sets the journey in motion or informs the reader that something is at stake. Don't feel you have to tell your reader everything at once. Keep them guessing and they'll be obliged to stick with the story to find out what happened next.

Pursuing a dream involves hope and fears, anticipations and disappointments, obstacles, achievements, failures, and success. These are the results of your protagonist's choices, actions, encounters, and history and can be used as elements of your plot.

VOICES OF THE MASTERS

Caroline Knapp's memoir, *Drinking: A Love Story,* begins as follows:

I drank.

I drank Fumé Blanc at the Ritz-Carlton Hotel, and I drank double shots of Johnnie.

Walker Black on the rocks at the dingy Chinese restaurant across the street from my office, and I drank at home. For a long time I drank expensive red wine, and I learned to appreciate the subtle differences between a silky Merlot and a tart Cabernet Sauvignon and a soft, earthy Beaucastel from the south of France, but I never really cared about those nuances because, honestly, they were beside the point. Toward the end I kept two bottles of Cognac in my house: the bottle for show, which I kept on the counter, and the real bottle, which I kept in the back of a cupboard beside an old toaster. The level of liquid in the show bottle was fairly consistent, decreasing by an inch or so, perhaps less, each week. The liquid in the real bottle disappeared quickly, sometimes within days. I was living alone at the time, when I did this, but I did it anyway and it didn't occur to me not to: it was always important to maintain appearances.

Caroline Knapp, who died in 2002, honed her writing style as a newspaper feature writer and columnist. "The key," she once said, "has less to do with insight than with willingness, the former being relatively useless without the latter."

In this opening paragraph, we quickly appreciate that Knapp's unhealthy relationship with alcohol is what sets her journey in motion. Her objective has been implied—to confront this addiction and stop drinking. The middle of Knapp's memoir shows the protagonist striving to attain her objective. She encounters obstacles along the way. These antagonists seek to prevent the protagonist from achieving her goal. The inclusion of these difficulties help to build tension as the story nears its climax.

In Chapter 10 of Knapp's *Drinking* we encounter denial, one of the narrator's antagonists:

> *You often hear in AA meetings that denial is the disease of alcoholism, not just its primary symptom, and it's not hard to see why. Denial is what keeps you in there, keeps you entrenched, keeps your feet glued to the floor. Denial can make your drinking feel as elusive and changeable as Proteus, capable of altering form in the blink of an eye. Every time an active alcoholic looks at his or her drinking, it's shifted into something else, something that makes it seem acceptable.*

Denial is just one of the many factors that makes it difficult for Knapp to quit. She illustrates by example the ways she denied her problem so that the drinking would continue. This playing out of cause and effect contributes to the momentum of her story and helps develop her plot.

As we approach a story's end, the protagonist must be shown to come close to resolution, experiencing some kind of final confrontation before she succeeds or fails in her quest. In Knapp's memoir she hits bottom before she seeks help. Though already sober at the time of writing the book (so the reader knows the narrator succeeds on her mission), the act of "hitting bottom" is an effective storytelling tool. It creates tension for the reader, particularly as Knapp experiences a tragedy—her parents' deaths—before being given one last chance to sober up.

In this story, the protagonist opts for that one last chance by checking herself into rehab. In the final chapter the reader gets to witness the narrator's sobriety. We are told of her struggle to stay sober, her new understanding of her father, the insight she has gained into her drinking problem, and her assessment of the life she must live if she is to avoid drinking.

Alternative plot structures

Though the classic story structure is commonly used in fiction and memoir, it is not your only choice. Your life story might be revealed in an exchange of letters or in a collection of stories or vignettes. It's possible to alternate between two stories—perhaps one in the present and the other in the past. Or if you're writing about a relationship, you might alternate between your individual story and the story of the relationship. Even if you employ a beginning, middle, and end in the classic sense, you might choose to weave in and out of time, to use flash forwards and flashbacks as a way of stringing your memories together into a narrative.

> **Ensure that your story contains some kind of constant progression.**

No matter what structure you choose, as a writer you must ensure that your story contains some kind of constant progression, interspersed with conflicts, and some kind of movement toward a resolution, whether it's what your protagonist achieves or not.

Your story's progression can follow your protagonist's growing self-awareness—his struggle to learn about himself as he reexamines his past. The efforts to accept himself, the choices he has made, or his past can serve as obstacles in the plot. If you're writing about a relationship, a career path, or a trip, consider who or what gets in the way. No matter what your protagonist's journey, it's important to make sure you include complications—these help create tension for the reader. And since the protagonist needs to undergo some kind of transformation, be sure to reflect upon how your journey led to change.

Description

Details enable the reader to experience the story. They help him picture the visuals, summon up the sounds, feel the sensations, go through the emotions, and imagine the scents and tastes. Without the use of accurate description to describe a character or set a scene, a story isn't grounded: It's like a research paper without facts. When attempting to paint a picture of a specific moment or scene, one might approach this task as if literally painting a picture. By including only the most relevant information within the story's framework, one can narrow the reader's focus. Look at the composition, how the setting relates to the characters, and what other contributing factors the reader/viewer has to consider. How might you make the scene more real? Have you given equal attention to all the five senses, not just visually describing the scene, but also depicting the sounds, textures, scents, and tastes, that are most relevant to the protagonist's experience?

VOICES OF THE MASTERS

Denis Johnson, a fiction writer who's also a poet, makes vivid use of description in his short-story collection *Jesus' Son*. In "A Car Crash while Hitchhiking," the narrator, a hitchhiker, surveys the scene of the car crash he has just survived.

> Before too long there were cars backed up for a ways at either end of the bridge, and headlights giving a night-game atmosphere to the steaming rubble, and ambulances and cop cars nudging through so that the air pulsed with color. I didn't talk to anyone. My secret was that in this short while I had gone from being the president of this tragedy to being a faceless onlooker at a gory wreck. At some point an officer learned that I was one of the passengers, and took my statement. I don't remember any of this, except that he told me, "Put out your cigarette." We paused in our conversation to watch the dying man being loaded into the ambulance. He was still alive, still dreaming obscenely. The blood ran off him in strings. His knees jerked and his head rattled.

It's not hard to picture the scene: the headlights, the steam, the red lights. The notion of blood running in strings is particularly striking—it's clear, accurate, and unusual.

The words and images that you use to convey your story to the reader are part of what makes your tale unique. Be playful in your use of description, take risks, and avoid the shorthand of cliché. If a simile or metaphor seems awkward on rereading, lose it and think of something better.

WRITERS WORKSHOP

Get your facts straight. If your reader doesn't trust that your words are true (especially in a memoir), she will lose interest and put down your book. How can you avoid this scenario? Be specific. Do research. Use proper names when necessary.

- Don't use clichés (his heart skipped a beat; she had a heart of stone). It's lazy language and will immediately tell the reader that you haven't done your work.

- Do make your descriptions suit the mood of the character or scene. Is it a car, or is it a "blood-red Cadillac"? Is it a bed, or is it "an unmade bed, twin-sized, its pillow stained with sweat"? Was it a rainy day, or was it "a day of monsoonlike rain with clouds so low and dark she'd forgotten there was a sun"? If you can describe something in a way that's never been described before, your reader won't forget it.

- Do use similes to compare one thing to another: "The children's bodies bobbed in the lake like apples."

- Do use metaphors to keep your description vital: "Her smile was a curse."

- Do use personification to give inanimate objects humanlike qualities: "The leaves fell like tears from the tree."

- Do employ hyperbole—an exaggeration so outrageous it's immediately recognized as such—to make a point: "Her scream shattered the windows, the glasses, all mirrors, and my thoughts."

- Don't be wordy. Use a limited number of strong adjectives and adverbs to describe your characters and settings, not lists of weak words.

- Don't leave room for the reader to interpret. Make your detail ring true; it shouldn't come across as abstract.

When it comes to character development or plot, your reader should be allowed space to make her own interpretations, but when it comes to describing, it's your job to make sure that the reader understands exactly what you mean. For example, you could say, "The music was loud," but it wouldn't mean much—loud has different meanings for an 80-year-old man and a teenage boy. But if you were to write, "The music came through the window and rattled the picture frames on the wall," then the reader would know exactly how loud you mean.

- Don't overdo it. If you give too much detail, your reader will lose sight of the story. Think of descriptions as ingredients in a recipe—there are infinite combinations, but not all of them will taste good.

Showing vs. Telling

When you show your reader your characters, you allow her to judge the characters for herself by presenting facts and observations about them. When you tell the reader about your characters, you are forcing your opinions of them onto her, so you do not allow her to form her own opinion. Readers like to feel smart. They like to make connections and figure out complexities without being told what or how to think. If a writer too often tries to give readers her interpretation and tell them what to think, they are likely to feel cornered and start to lose confidence in the writer.

Revealing your characters

How can a writer show his characters? Look back to pages 28–29 and 102–105 and review the notes you have made on the characters in your life story. You can show a character with a physical description of his looks, his gestures, his physical presence, and what he's wearing. Is he comfortable in his clothes, or does he look out of place in a suit? How does she communicate with others? Does she make direct eye and physical contact (with confidence) or does she stand at a distance, with her arms across her chest, refusing to meet another character's eye? Are his gestures conservative or grand? Do they change much with his emotions and do they match his voice? Does she have any habits, such as bouncing her knee, smoking, or tucking her hair behind her ears? All of these traits reveal something about a character and, when put together, will help create a whole person on the page.

You don't need to be shy in your description. As a writer, you're free to go right up to your characters— to notice the delicate lines at the corners of your mother's mouth or pupils that dilate like ink on a blotter. Don't stop your story to demand that the reader notices these details. Feed them in gradually.

If one of your characters is happy, show your readers by describing the way she kicks her legs through the water, the dimples when she smiles, and the sun's warmth on her skin.

VOICES OF THE MASTERS

Augusten Burroughs's memoir *Running with Scissors* provides a scene in which an argument takes place between his parents. Note what you learn about his mother's character from her exchange with Burroughs's father, based on her actions and her words.

"You infantile tyrant," my mother shouted from her position on the sofa, legs folded up beneath her. "You goddamn bastard. You'd like nothing more than to see me slit my wrists." She absently twisted the tassel on her long crocheted vest....

She stood up from the sofa and walked slowly across the white shag carpeting, as if finding her mark on a soundstage. "I'm hysterical?" she asked in a smooth, low voice, "You think this is hysterical?" She laughed theatrically, throwing her head back. "Oh you poor bastard. You lousy excuse for a man." She stood next to him, leaning her back against the teak bookcase. "You're so repressed you mistake creative passion for hysterics. And don't you see? This is how you're killing me." She closed her eyes and made her Edith Piaf face.

The emotional content of the mother's speech is clearly disconnected from her actions—threatening to slit her wrists while twisting the tassel on her long crocheted vest, for example. Each action is described in the manner of a stage direction, suggesting that her speech, too, lacks sincerity—though this is shown to the reader rather than being told to her outright.

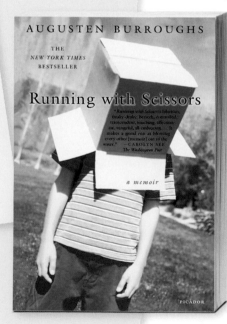

What your characters do and say

A character's actions, when closely observed, will reveal the most about him. Do your characters' actions convey something other than their words? Consider every action from the small to the grand. How does she walk across the room, make a cup of coffee, or pick up the phone? How does he react under pressure or in a moment of crisis? Do different characters inspire different behaviors? Do your characters reveal emotions as soon as they feel them, or do they try to hide them?

> **A character's actions, when closely observed, will reveal the most about him.**

Dialogue, along with the actions of your characters, is what sets a scene. But a dialogue is more than words; the way in which a character speaks, pauses, and falls silent will reveal much about who he is. Look for inconsistencies in your character's voice and ask what they mean. What reveals most about her emotions: her tone of voice, her words, or her body language?

Burroughs's follow-up, Dry: A Memoir, is an account of his alcoholism. Acknowledging one of the inherent difficulties of memoir writing, he includes this note: "This memoir is based on my experiences over a ten year period.... Certain episodes are imaginative re-creation, and those episodes are not intended to portray actual events."

Point of View and Voice

The subject of your story, the personality of your narrator/protagonist, and the nature of his struggle will help determine your voice. Whether your life story is funny, serious, or sad, it needs to run as a continuous thread throughout your account and can be indirectly communicated to the reader through your voice. Look for the voice in the works of your favorite writers: how present they are, as narrators, on the page. The key to mastering voice is letting it evolve naturally while maintaining consistency.

Establishing voice

Voice is your presence on the page. It's the personality of the writer/narrator—her tone. It's how you come across, how you present yourself; it's what glues the words together and turns them into a story.

The tricky thing about voice is that it can't be forced. You have to find your voice naturally, over time, by writing. You shouldn't focus on developing a voice, but rather on the story you are telling; a voice will develop on its own. Once you find your voice in the story, you can go back and revise what you've written to further develop it.

> ### You have to find your voice naturally, over time, by writing.

One element that contributes to voice is the tone or the emotional feel of the story—is the narrator angry, happy, confused, frustrated, or sad? Other factors include the writer's diction or word choice; his syntax or sentence structure; and paragraph length. Do not make a conscious effort to develop any of these features in your first few drafts. Write your story and see how the narrator develops his story. You may think you have a

Once you identify your story, you'll be able to determine the chunk of time over which it spans. Whether the life story that you are writing covers a few generations or a few years, this time period will affect your pacing and how you choose to manipulate time.

certain reaction to a situation, but your writer's voice may have another story to tell.

Once you've scripted a first, second, or third draft and can detect the presence of a voice, you can rework your story to emphasize this. Make a note of how your protagonist's observations contribute to the story's tone. You can also consider descriptions of weather, light, atmospheric details (paint peeling from the walls versus a freshly painted room), sentence length (short, choppy sentences to emphasize an angry tone), and word choice. How you describe something should imply something more than the object you're attempting to illustrate.

VOICES OF THE MASTERS

J. M. Coetzee, the South African novelist, won his second Booker Prize for fiction with his novel *Disgrace*. Unlike most memoirs, which are written in the first person, using "I" Coetzee wrote his memoir *Boyhood*, in the third person. The following extract is taken from the chilling opening chapter, in which his mother tries to escape her restlessness at home by teaching herself to ride a bike but is mocked by Coetzee and his father until she finally gives up.

> *The memory of his mother on her bicycle does not leave him. She pedals away up Poplar Avenue, escaping from him, escaping towards her own desire. He does not want her to go. He does not want her to have a desire of her own. He wants her always to be in the house, waiting for him when he comes home. He does not often gang up with his father against her: his whole inclination is to gang up with her against his father. But in this case he belongs with the men.*

Coetzee's use of "he" effectively severs the connection between the narrator and his protagonist, so that the narrator is not a character in the story. Writing in this way may have given Coetzee some distance on the emotional experience of his past, perhaps making it easier for him to hold nothing back.

James Baldwin, an American essayist and novelist, writes about his relationship with his father, a preacher, in his essay, "Notes of a Native Son." The following excerpt is the essay's opening paragraph. Take note of how Baldwin sets the tone.

> *On the twenty-ninth of July, in 1943, my father died. On the same day, a few hours later, his last child was born. Over a month before this, while all our energies were concentrated in waiting for these events, there had been, in Detroit, one of the bloodiest race riots of the century. A few hours after my father's funeral, while he lay in state in the undertaker's chapel, a race riot broke out in Harlem. On the morning of the third of August, we drove my father to the graveyard through a wilderness of smashed plate glass.*

Baldwin's voice in this extract is an angry one. He chooses what information he gives the reader carefully—starkly juxtaposing details of the political situation of the time with the facts of his father's death to tell us something of their relationship. Without being told directly, we are certain it was not a happy one.

James Baldwin was born in Harlem in 1924 and started writing at an early age: "I didn't know how I would use my mind, or even if I could, but that was the only thing I had to use."

Setting

The setting of a story is the place in which it occurs and the time at which it happens: the time of day, month, and year, and the wider, historical context. What was happening in the world, in culture and society, at the time of your story? Place includes the big picture and the small—country, city, village, or town—where your story is set. Is it a mining town, a mountain village, or an industrial city? Place includes inside and out. What interior spaces feature in your story? Dark bars, airy barns, or stuffy classrooms? How do these settings affect your characters and the choices they make?

Considering the environment

Remember that setting is anything that contributes to the environment: the weather, the light, the feel of the air, the ambient sound, and the textures of the surfaces with which the characters interact (plush couches or hard-backed chairs). When you write about setting, think about how it affects your characters—are they comfortable in their space or ill at ease? Is the setting an antagonist, which somehow prevents the protagonist from achieving her goals (for example, a small town that suffocates her creativity)? How does the setting make the characters feel? Is your protagonist happiest with her family at home or when she's alone? Considering exactly how your characters interact with their environment—a woman obliged to stay in a job she dislikes, or a boy prevented from going outside because of a snowstorm—will help create drama.

Setting as a character

Joseph Mitchell was a New York reporter and feature writer who also wrote four books, now published collectively as *Up in the Old Hotel and Other Stories*. The extract opposite, from the first essay of his first book, *McSorley's Wonderful Saloon*, is a portrait of a

> Picture the flickering shadows and cobwebs that contribute to the sleepy atmosphere.

When you describe the setting, remember to include as many details as possible. Indeed, the setting can act as a character in your story. Joseph Mitchell used the setting of a saloon to great effect in McSorley's Wonderful Saloon.

place. The author's choice of protagonist is not a person but a bar. He includes dates, but the items within the room also offer historical context. You can picture the flickering shadows and cobwebs that contribute to the sleepy atmosphere. The people are described not as individuals, but as fixtures, as constant as the irregular clocks.

VOICES OF THE MASTERS

Joseph Mitchell, a New York reporter and the author of *Up in the Old Hotel and Others Stories*, effectively portrays the atmosphere in this 88-year-old saloon in Greenwich Village.

McSorley's occupies the ground floor of a red-brick tenement at 15 Seventh Street, just off Cooper Square, where the Bowery ends. It was opened in 1854 and is the oldest saloon in New York City. In 88 years it has had four owners—an Irish immigrant, his son, a retired policeman, and his daughter—and all of them have been opposed to change. It is equipped with electricity, but the bar is stubbornly illuminated with a pair of gas lamps, which flicker fitfully and throw shadows on the low, cobwebby ceiling each time someone opens the street door. There is no cash register. Coins are dropped in soup bowls—one for nickels, one for dimes, one for quarters, and one for halves—and bills are kept in a rosewood cashbox. It is a drowsy place; the bartenders never make a needless move, the customers nurse their mugs of ale, and the three clocks on the walls have not been in agreement for many years. The clientele is motley. It includes mechanics from the many garages in the neighborhood, salesmen from the restaurant-supply houses on Cooper Square, truck-drivers from Wanamaker's, interns from Bellevue, students from Cooper Union, and clerks from the row of second-hand bookshops just north of Astor Place. The backbone of the clientele, however, is a rapidly thinning group of crusty old men, predominantly Irish, who have been drinking there since they were youths and now have a proprietary feeling about the place.

Anne Frank was 13 years old when, while in hiding from the Nazis during World War II, she wrote *The Diary of a Young Girl*. In this excerpt she succeeds in painting a picture of the airless interior of her hiding place and in illustrating her family's imprisonment.

Since the vacuum cleaner's broken, I have to take an old brush to the rug every night. The window's closed, the light's on, the stove's burning, and there I am brushing away at the rug…. Mother got a headache from the thick clouds of dust whirling around the room, Margot's new Latin dictionary was caked with dirt, and Pim grumbled that the floor didn't look any different anyway. Small thanks for my pains.

We've decided that from now on the stove is going to be lit at seven-thirty on Sunday mornings instead of five-thirty. I think it's risky. What will the neighbors think of our smoking chimney?

It's the same with the curtains. Ever since we first went into hiding, they've been tacked firmly to the windows. Sometimes one of the ladies or gentlemen can't resist the urge to peek outside. The result: a storm of reproaches. The response: "Oh, nobody will notice." That's how every act of carelessness begins and ends. No one will notice, no one will hear, no one will pay the least bit of attention. Easy to say, but is it true?

Visual Representations of Place

You may want to include some images of the places that are featured in your story. Whether you choose to use personal photographs, sketches, collages, photographs cut out of newspapers, postcards, or paintings, these illustrations can be used to shed light on your narrative and develop a sense of place for the reader.

Creating a setting through images

What places play a significant role in your life story? Do you want to include a picture of your current home, your city or town, your neighborhood, your garden, your vacation spots, the path of your weekly walks, your childhood home, your backyard, or your local park? Consider what medium best suits your creativity and your subject—black-and-white film, watercolors, or pictures cut from magazines. What mood or message do you wish to convey? Your choice of colors and medium will help reveal this. Think about whether you want to present your setting in broader terms (by offering historical and cultural context) or to keep the references small, in relation to a specific individual or moment. Would it help to include people for reference or scale? If people are included, how do they interact with this space and what meaning can you take from this?

Taking pictures

When photographing, try to use natural light. Flash tends to wash out or light things too evenly and, unless you really know what you're doing, can detract from the atmosphere. Think of the mood created in a photograph shot with natural daylight streaming in through the windows. If the place you are photographing is dark and needs a long exposure, put the camera on a tripod. If your subject is still, you can expose it for as long as necessary. Bracket your photographs (take multiple

Photography is an excellent medium for capturing visual representations of place. When possible, take photographs in natural light and at different exposures to ensure that you create the look, mood, and atmosphere you desire.

photographs with some of the settings slightly modified); take the same picture at different exposures to ensure you have the one you want.

If taking photographs isn't an option, that's fine. There are many ways to depict the settings that have affected and influenced your life. If you do some research, you may be able to find some old photographs, or you can create your own images, emphasizing in a painting or collage the aspects that were relevant to you. Your depictions don't have to be exact. What you choose to illustrate and include is informative in itself.

Collage

Romare Bearden was an American artist who painted and drew, photographed and designed, and created experimental collages, for which he is well known. Having grown up in Harlem during the Harlem Renaissance (a flowering of African-American social thought), Bearden bore witness to and accepted the influences of the many great jazz musicians, poets, performers, and visual artists of the time. In many of his collage works, such as *The Block*, shown here, Bearden depicted the cityscape as well as the African-American community that inhabited it.

> He captures the variety of individuals who inhabit the neighborhood, the old and young, at work and at play.

A six-panel collage depicting a single block in Harlem, *The Block* celebrates the public theater of the streets and the private lives lived behind windows and walls. Bearden visualizes hope in the angels that lift the deceased toward the heavens from the funeral home below, and hopelessness in the homeless man asleep on the sidewalk. He captures the variety of individuals who inhabit the neighborhood, the old and young, at work and at play. In this collage we can imagine the sounds of the block and the lives lived. The artist has provided context, and left much for the viewer to imagine.

Bearden once said of this work: "When I sketched this block, I was looking at a particular street, but as I translated it into visual form it became something else. I lost the literalness and moved into where my imagination took me. I x-rayed the facades with my imagination."

Theme

Even if you haven't identified your life story's themes in the planning stage, themes will inevitably begin to emerge once you've been writing for a while. How will you recognize a theme when it presents itself? Remember that a theme is the overall point of the story, its message. Your story should have a universal theme—a message that all individuals can relate to regardless of culture or age, such as the desire to love and be loved, becoming an adult, or overcoming loss. It should also have a unique sub-theme, one that makes your story uniquely yours or provides an original way of perceiving your situation, which enables you to tell a story as it's never been told before—such as your fear of heights and the various ways in which you confront this fear.

Sticking to your themes

Themes help link pieces of a story together, to give it purpose and a sense of direction. Once you've identified your themes, you will have a much clearer idea of what to include and what to leave out of your life story. If a certain life experience doesn't tie in with your overall theme, don't include it.

You may have decided your themes in advance and be writing with them in mind, but produce a story with a focus you had not originally intended. Themes tend to emerge of their own accord, with life forces of their own. If you discover a theme that you hadn't anticipated, you can backtrack and rearrange your story to enhance it.

Don't overwhelm your reader with the obvious by stating and restating the theme in your story. A theme should be something your reader recognizes or gradually comes to realize over time. A character may hint at it, or it could emerge as a result of your protagonist's actions. No matter how you choose to reveal your theme, it should be linked to your protagonist's goals and to the plot, which is the result of your character's actions. Ask yourself how your protagonist's objective is related to your story's theme. There should be a connection between the two.

If a particular fear is one of your greatest obstacles in life (i.e., fear of intimacy, fear of ambition, fear of loss), then turn this fear into one of your life-story themes. Write about it as you would any relationship—how it began and your desire to change.

VOICES OF THE MASTERS

Vladimir Nabokov's *Speak, Memory* is a collection of memories from his childhood, and its universal theme could be said to be coming of age. In the following passage, Nabokov begins by sharing with the reader a specific moment from his life that occurred when he was a child of five.

> I had an even earlier association with that war. One afternoon at the beginning of the same year, in our St. Petersburg house, I was led down from the nursery into my father's study to say how-do-you-do to a friend of the family, General Kuropatkin. His thickset, uniform-encased body creaking slightly, he spread out to amuse me a handful of matches, on the divan where he was sitting, placed ten of them end to end to make a horizontal line, and said, "This is the sea in calm weather." Then he tipped up each pair so as to turn the straight line into a zigzag—and that was "a stormy sea." He scrambled the matches and was about to do, I hoped, a better trick when we were interrupted. His aide-de-camp was shown in and said something to him.... That day, he had been ordered to assume supreme command of the Russian Army in the Far East.
>
> This incident had a special sequel fifteen years later, when at a certain point of my father's flight from Bolshevick-held St. Petersburg to southern Russia he was accosted while crossing a bridge, by an old man who looked like a gray-bearded peasant in his sheepskin coat. He asked my father for a light. The next moment each recognized the other. I hope old Kuropatkin, in his rustic disguise, managed to evade Soviet imprisonment, but that is not the point. What pleases me is the evolution of the match theme: those magic ones he had shown me had been trifled with and mislaid, and his armies had also vanished, and everything had fallen through, like my toy trains.... The following of such thematic designs through one's life should be, I think, the true purpose of autobiography.

Using an object, the match, Nabokov links the first experience to the second. The match bridges the passing of time, which is a subtheme of Nabokov's memoir. Everyone who becomes an adult passes through childhood, which makes this a universal theme, but the awareness of it passing is a theme specific to Nabokov.

Self-reflection takes time and digging deep is an integral part of the memoir-writing experience—reflecting on behavior and choices, upon your impact on others, and upon the effects others have had on you.

The Writer's Remove

The memoir writer should not judge his characters or himself on the page. While you will never wholly eradicate your emotional reaction or connection to an experience (and you shouldn't strive to), before you start writing your life story, you need to ensure that enough time has passed to enable you to write clearly, without an excess of jealousy, sadness, rage, pride, or pity clouding your judgment.

Self-reflection is the key ingredient here. Your aim is to convey your experience intimately so that the reader feels she is in your skin, and to view your own life objectively, with enough remove to refrain from judgments. No matter how much someone has wronged you or how great the deed you may have done, never accuse or gloat. Your job as a writer is to craft your story and present the facts so that the reader may judge for himself.

This also means being able to accept fault for when you were wrong and to recognize your contribution to any situation, no matter how great or horrific. Just as you don't want to blame others for mishaps or gloat over your successes, you don't want to blame yourself unreasonably for something that was not your fault.

> **Your job as a writer is to craft your story and present the facts without judgment.**

Reining it in

How much is too much? Compare the act of writing your life story to telling a story to an audience at a cocktail party. How do you feel when you are forced to surrender your ears to a speaker who goes on and on about himself and how great he is, or whines about how miserable he is for having failed to accomplish his dreams? What do you see when you scan the audience—how many eyes rolled, how many yawns and watches checked? Think about how much information you need for the audience to grasp your point, get it across, and leave it at that.

This isn't to say you should edit yourself as you write; as discussed on page 87, you need to let everything hang out in your first draft. However, by the time you've come to recognize your protagonist's objective and your story's themes, you should be thinking about what to include and what to leave out.

Self-reflection takes time, and digging deep is an integral part of the memoir-writing experience— reflecting on behavior and choices, your impact on others, and the effects others have had on you.

VOICES OF THE MASTERS

Malcolm X, in *The Autobiography of Malcolm X,* writes about "the first major turning point" of his life in a scene with his English teacher, Mr. Ostrowski.

> He told me, "Malcolm, you ought to be thinking about a career. Have you been giving it thought?"
>
> The truth is, I hadn't. I never have figured out why I told him, "Well, yes, sir, I've been thinking I'd like to be a lawyer...."
>
> Mr. Ostrowski looked surprised, I remember, and leaned back in his chair and clasped his hands behind his head. He kind of half-smiled and said, "Malcolm, one of life's first needs is for us to be realistic. Don't misunderstand me, now. We all here like you, you know that. But you've got to be realistic about being a nigger. A lawyer—that's no realistic goal for a nigger. You need to think about something you can be. You're good with your hands—making things. Everybody admires your carpentry shop work. Why don't you plan on carpentry? People like you as a person—you'd get all kinds of work."
>
> The more I thought afterwards about what he said, the more uneasy it made me. It just kept treading around in my mind.
>
> What made it really begin to disturb me was Mr. Ostrowski's advice to others in my class—all of them white.... They all reported that Mr. Ostrowski had encouraged whatever they had wanted. Yet nearly none of them had earned marks equal to mine.
>
> It was a surprising thing that I had never thought of it that way before, but I realized that whatever I wasn't, I was smarter than nearly all of those white kids. But apparently I was still not intelligent enough, in their eyes, to become whatever I wanted to be.
>
> It was then that I began to change—inside.

As angry as the experience may have made the narrator, Malcolm X doesn't allow this emotion to dominate the page. Instead, he uses the scene to show how this experience leads him to change. He presents the facts and constructs a picture that displays his feelings—frustration, hurt, and surprise. He gives the reader room to breathe in the scene and doesn't crowd him with his take on it.

Form

At some point in the process, you need to consider form—the format in which you want your life story to appear. Do you want to tell your life story in letters, as a journal, a memoir, or as a collection of essays, vignettes, or short stories?

Experiment with form

If you're not sure what format is right for you, try a few on for size. Take one experience and present it in different forms, seeing which best suits your topic and natural style. If you can't decide, combine two formats. Your life story could consist of a collection of letters and snapshots or be a memoir that includes journal entries. You might start out writing a personal essay and find your story expanding into a memoir. Ultimately, it's your life story—you can make up your own rules about how best to convey it.

Telling your story through correspondence

If you opt to tell your story in letters (or e-mails), you need to decide if you want to include your side of a single exchange, your side of numerous exchanges, your correspondence with one individual, or with many. Whatever you choose, you must ensure that your letters tell a story and span a certain theme or period of time.

VOICES OF THE MASTERS

Dylan Thomas, the Welsh poet, corresponded regularly with his wife and lovers; his love letters to them are published collectively as *The Love Letters of Dylan Thomas*. The following extract is taken from a letter to his wife, Caitlin, written from New York.

> *And now it must look to you, my Cat, as though I am enjoying myself here. I'm not. It's nightmare, night & day; there was never such a place; I would never get used to the speed, the noise, the utter indifference of the crowds, the frightening politeness of the intellectuals, and, most of all, those huge phallic towers, up & up & up, hundreds of floors, into the impossible sky. I feel so terrified of this place, I hardly dare to leave my hotelroom—luxurious—until Brinnin or someone calls for me. Everybody uses the telephone all the time: it is like breathing: it is now nine o'clock in the morning, & I've had six calls: all from people whose names I did not catch to invite me to a little poity at an address I had not idea of.*

In this, as in all his letters, Thomas displays his feeling for the receiver and his reactions to his environment and current situation in the same vein as a journal entry.

The short story or essay

If you want to dissect your life story into small, digestible chunks, you could follow in the steps of Abigail Thomas, whose *Safekeeping: Some True Stories from a Life* offers glimpses into her world. Usually not more than a page or two long, each of her stories capture a small moment in time like a photograph.

The personal essay is another format you might choose to tell your life story. Its restricted length forces the writer to limit her focus, something that some writers find difficult. A good example of this can be found in the essays in Caroline Knapp's *The Merry Recluse: A Life in Essays*. These cover a range of topics, such as friendship and love, addictions, shyness, and loneliness.

Abigail Thomas's piece, "Io Keep Him Company," though only two sentences long, paints a portrait of her parents' relationship.

> *The night my father fell and couldn't get up and my mother couldn't get him up not being strong enough and it was four in the morning, they didn't want to disturb anyone at that hour by telephoning for help. So she lay down beside him on the floor and stayed with him until morning.*

It's a short passage, limited to a specific moment, but Thomas manages to convey strong feelings of love and tenderness. She reveals much about the state of her parents and their relationship, and the fact that she chooses to write about this scene reveals a lot about herself. There is a sense of awe in the author's awareness of her parents' bond with each other.

Natalia Ginzburg, a celebrated Italian writer, uses self-deprecating humor to explore her relationship with her husband, in her essay, *He and I.*

> *He always feels hot, I always feel cold. In the summer when he is really hot he does nothing but complain about how hot he feels. He is irritated if he sees me put a jumper on in the evening.*
>
> *He speaks several languages well; I do not speak any well. He manages—in his own way—to speak even the languages that he doesn't know.*
>
> *He has an excellent sense of direction, I have none at all. After one day in a foreign city he can move about in it as thoughtlessly as a butterfly. I get lost in my own city....*
>
> *He loves museums, and I will go if I am forced to but with an unpleasant sense of effort and duty. He loves libraries and I hate them.*
>
> *He loves traveling, unfamiliar foreign cities, restaurants. I would like to stay at home all the time and never move.*

Ginzburg's wry look at their differences is typical of her understated writing, and of her unsentimental approach to family relationships.

Structure

Your approach to developing structure, which constitutes the shape of your plot—the frame upon which you hang your story that helps to direct how your story unfolds—will depend upon where you are with your story. If you've written a series of short stories or scenes and would like to create a memoir, then you need to consider how you might best string these separate episodes together. Even if you only have a list of memories based on specific individuals, scenes, or events, you can consider putting together an outline for your life story (see below) and using it to help you create and/or shape your plot.

Constructing an outline

Revisiting the idea of a time line (see pages 26–27), let's look in depth at how you can build on this device and construct an outline. An outline maps out your story and needn't be chronological. You can jump back and forth through time as long as there is some kind of thread to link the scenes together. You might be compiling a collection of stories from your working life as a nurse, for example, and find it most effective to place them in an order that allows you to compare similar dilemmas you have faced and how they were resolved. Alternatively, you might choose to jump between generations of your family history but anchor your scenes with a family heirloom, like an old piano or jewelry box. You may find it helpful to try outlining your favorite memoir first to see how the story is constructed.

My graduation

In love

Our special day

Constructing an outline will enable you to visualize how one passage, scene, or chapter should flow into the next, ensuring that all transitions are made smoothly.

WRITERS WORKSHOP

Vivian Gornick's *Fierce Attachments* is a memoir that is divided by scenes rather than chapters. For the sake of demonstrating story structure, the first few pages can be outlined as follows:

I   Apartment hallway

II   Narrator at 8 years old with her mother

III   Meets neighbor Mrs. Drucker

IV   Who sleeps with her despicable husband so she won't have to work

V   Tenement in the Bronx

VI   A building full of women (or so the narrator recalls)

VII   Who acted as if they knew themselves, but didn't

VIII   Who influenced the narrator

IX   It's taken her 30 years to understand how

X   Narrator walking with mother in New York City streets

XI   Recalling the neighbors and their volatile yet dependent relationships with their husbands

XII   Including Cessa, a grown woman beaten for cutting her own hair

XIII   Narrator's analysis of her relationship with her mother

XIV   Hot and cold; temperamental, yet binding

XV   They walk and often discuss the past

XVI   Mom recalls when her Uncle Sol tried to molest her

XVII   Narrator questions why mom was silent when he approached

XVIII   Narrator and mom don't speak for a month

Each Roman numeral represents a new section. Each new section brings the reader to a different place or a different location in time. Gornick often flashes back and forward through time, using theme as a thread to connect the various scenes.

Like wet clothes on a line, the events in your story need to be strung together and hung on a supporting structure. Analyze how other authors have organized their material in order to build, explore, and conclude their stories.

Examine this outline and try to identify the dominant themes. Clearly the memoir is about the lives of women; not just the tenement building full of women, but more specifically the narrator and her mother. What do the relationships have in common? From this outline you pick up a shared sense of dissatisfaction, a struggle for power, and finally, submission. To whom do the women submit? Men obviously play the dominant roles; the women are trapped.

The structure continues like this, moving between scenes and reflections, intercut with expository writings, all of which serve as the building blocks of Gornick's life story. By the end of the memoir, we see how these women influenced her life and witness the narrator's coming to terms with and understanding her experiences with men and her relationship with her mother. The reader's impression may be that Gornick simply let her life story flow out of her, but in reality even true stories need to be tethered to a coherent framework.

> To maximize tension, you might expand time or slow it down.

Manipulating time

The structure of your story helps determine your story's momentum—the way it moves forward, propelling your protagonist's plight. Even if the structure of your story is chronological, you will have to think about pacing and how to control the passing of time in order to elevate the stakes for your protagonist and keep the reader's interest. How do you want to construct your story? Do you want to present your events in chronological order or do you want to work with flashbacks and flash forwards? Pacing is the manipulation of time.

There will be moments when you need to condense time—when nothing really happens for five years, for example—and moments when you need to expand it to take in a significant event. If you want to maximize tension, you might expand time or slow it down so that the reader can linger on your every word. With a significant event, you might want to stretch it out over pages so that the reader has the opportunity to absorb every detail. It's perfectly acceptable to spend six pages on an event that took five minutes and to cover a year in a paragraph.

Time is putty in your hands. You can even stop the clock ticking and describe a scene as if frozen for eternity, if it helps your story. You're in control: If nothing interesting happened after breakfast, don't mention it, just fast-forward to when something did.

VOICES OF THE MASTERS

Harriet Jacobs's *Incidents in the Life of a Slave Girl* tells the story of the author as a slave. With her life's events recalled in a chronological order, Jacobs skips time when necessary, which keeps the momentum going, so that the reader witnesses action and change.

When I was nearly twelve years old, my kind mistress sickened and died….

I was sent to spend a week with my grandmother. I was now old enough to begin to think of the future; and again and again I asked myself what they would do with me. I felt sure I should never find another mistress so kind as the one who was gone. She had promised my dying mother that her children should never suffer for any thing; and when I remembered that, and recalled her many proofs of attachment to me, I could not help having some hopes that she had let me be free….

After a brief period of suspense, the will of my mistress was read, and we learned that she had bequeathed me to her sister's daughter, a child of five years old. So vanished our hopes….

Within a chronological structure, Jacobs creates tension with what she chooses to include. The disappointment she feels upon learning her fate prepares the reader for the difficult life that will follow.

Harriet Jacobs was born a slave in 1813. She escaped as a young woman to work as a nursemaid in New York, and began writing her autobiography. The content was considered almost too shocking for publication.

Momentum and change

The use of momentum enables the reader to witness some kind of change. The narrator/protagonist, either by flashing back to a time in life that reminds her of the present or by flashing forward to reveal a slice of the outcome, must undergo some kind of transformation. How you choose to demonstrate this change is up to you. You could show change in an individual or relationship through a series of letters, or indicate a shift in location in your scrapbook. No matter what method you choose, momentum is the key to keeping your reader engaged. If the information you include doesn't teach the reader anything new or further the story's momentum, eliminate it. If that means taking out a passage you're especially pleased with, so be it.

Inner Dialogue

Your life story will be all the more compelling if you are able to express yourself without holding back and worrying what others might think (see also pages 74–75). However, sometimes our memories freeze, leaving us unaware of why we feel a certain way or don't seem to feel anything at all. Any attempt to translate an experience such as this onto the page is unlikely to be successful as long as you are unaware of the effect this particular experience or individual has had on your life. Unfortunately, it's often necessary to revisit (or emotionally relive) an experience in order to communicate the situation effectively.

Free writing

How do you access your inner voice? Free writing can help and is great as a writing warm-up. "Free" means sitting before a blank sheet of paper or an empty computer screen and writing nonstop, whatever comes to mind. Even if you have to write "yes, no, yes, no, she is my friend, yes, no, yes, no, I am not mad," over and over, keep writing without stopping. The exercise is complete when you feel ready and able to access what's on your mind. Once you're "in the zone," you'll find that writing honestly about your life will not only improve your work but also teach you a lot about yourself.

Linking past and present

How many of your past experiences are tangled up in your present emotions? We all have inner conflicts born of previous experience: what we've been told to do versus what we truly desire. Sometimes we expose the conflict, and sometimes we try hard to keep it hidden. What cast of characters resides within your head? Are you afraid to reveal your innermost desires because of what other people might think? Do you sometimes resent the people you love for what they expect from you? As an adult, do you still place a higher priority on what your parents (or children or spouse) might think of your actions or decisions than on what you think yourself? If you can access these different characters, you will gain a better understanding of how you came to be the individual you are today.

For instance, have you ever experienced an unusually strong reaction to a situation that didn't warrant such a response? Examine this behavior— was your reaction linked to a similar incident in your past? You can use these past experiences as flashbacks in your story and let the reader make the link between memory and the present moment.

Free writing can be done anywhere, at any time— while waiting for a train or trying to sleep; or as a warm-up to loosen and stretch your inhibitions, memories, crafting capabilities, and the muscles you employ to write.

VOICES OF THE MASTERS

Marcel Proust recognized the need to search one's "inmost depths" when writing and exemplified it in his text. The following passage is taken from the extensive opening paragraph of *Time Regained* and describes a return visit to the neighborhood of Combray.

I was distressed to see how little I relived my early years. I found the Vivonne narrow and ugly alongside the towpath. Not that I noticed any great physical discrepancies from what I remembered. But, separated as I was by a whole lifetime from places I now happened to be passing through again, there was lacking between them and me that contiguity from which is born, even before we have perceived it, the immediate, delicious and total deflagration of memory. Having doubtless no very clear conception of its nature, I was saddened by the thought that my faculty of feeling and imagining things must have diminished since I no longer took any pleasure in these walks.... We chatted—very agreeably for me. Not without difficulty, however. In so many people, there are different strata which are not alike: the character of the father, then of the mother; one traverses first one, then the other. But, next day, the order of their superimposition is reversed.... I remember that, in the course of our conversations during these walks, on several occasions she [Gilberte] surprised me a great deal. The first time was when she said to me: "If you were not too hungry and if it was not so late, by taking that road to the left and then turning to the right, in less than a quarter of an hour we should be at Guermantes." It was as though she had said to me: "Turn to the left, then bear right, and you will touch the intangible, you will reach the inaccessibly remote tracts of which one never knows anything on this earth except the direction, except" (what I thought long ago to be all that I could ever know of Guermantes, and perhaps in a sense I had not been mistaken) "the 'way.'"

Here Proust addresses the concept of memory, of revisiting the route his protagonist once took as a child, only to find a lack of connection with his past, which the narrator fears has erased his capacity to feel. His friend, Gilberte, is composed of "different strata," a variety of personas who make her character whole. When she suggests revisiting Guermantes (his past), he hears her suggesting that they visit the unknown.

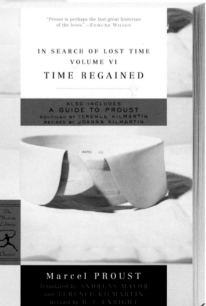

The sixth volume in Proust's great work In Remembrance of Times Past, Time Regained is concerned with the effects of the passing of time on perception and memory.

Writing Someone Else's Story

You can incorporate aspects of another person's story into your memoir, journal, or scrapbook by extracting their letters or diary entries (if you are lucky enough to have these). This can also be done by editing your personal interviews down to the most relevant, revealing, or interesting parts and including these in your text as dialogue, with or without quotation marks. If you are assembling a scrapbook, you might include excerpts from interviews or quotations alongside images of the individuals concerned. You could keep the theme of your text consistent by having different individuals answer similar questions, or choose a section of text that you feel best represents the individual being depicted.

When conducting an interview, think of how to best put your interviewee at ease—the more comfortable they are, the more information they will give you.

Interviewing another person

If you want to relate another person's story closely to your own, you might choose to include interview extracts that are either most relevant to your relationship or to the themes that are explored in your life story. You might even choose to include another person's interpretation of a similar situation or experience alongside, or alternating with, your own experience.

When transcribing dialogue from an interview, don't alter the speaker's words. It is acceptable to cut lines or sections that are not as interesting or relevant to the story you wish to tell, but if you do this, be careful not to manipulate your interviewee's thoughts or words.

> Be careful not to manipulate your interviewee's thoughts or words.

VOICES OF THE MASTERS

Nigel Nicolson was the son of British writers Harold Nicolson and Vita Sackville-West, who was one of Virginia Woolf's closest friends. In his biography of Woolf, Nicolson weaves his childhood experiences with the writer into her life story. *Virginia Woolf* begins with the following passage:

> In her childhood Virginia Woolf was a keen hunter of butterflies and moths. With her brothers and sister she would smear tree trunks with treacle to attract and capture the insects, and then pin their lifelike corpses to cork boards, their wings outspread. It was an interest that persisted into her adult life, and when she discovered that I too was a bug hunter, she insisted that we go hunting together in the fields around Long Barn, our house in Kent, two miles from Knole, my mother's birthplace. I was nine years old.

> One summer's afternoon when we were sweeping the tall grass with our nets and catching nothing, she suddenly paused, leaning on her bamboo cane as a savage might lean on his assegai, and said to me: "What's it like to be a child?" I, taken aback, replied, "Well, Virginia, you know what it's like. You've been a child yourself. I don't know what it's like to be you, because I've never been grown-up." It was the only occasion when I got the better of her dialectically.

Nicolson draws on his research to script the beginning of the first paragraph, then blends her life with his, linking the two together through their fondness for butterflies and moths, which leads to a scene where we learn something about each of the characters.

You don't have to attempt a full-fledged biography if you decide that you want to tell someone else's life story alongside your own. Choose the structure or form that best suits what research material you have, refrain from judgment, and depict your subject's life story as clearly and as honestly as you would want him or her to depict your own.

If you choose to tell someone else's life story alongside or within your own, you can expect to learn about yourself, your subject, and the dynamics of your relationship.

Writing About Food

Since eating is an essential part of everybody's life, you may want to make it the focus of your life story, or at least a theme. A food-focused travelogue could include photographs of the meals you ate, menus, recipes, restaurant reviews, and food product labels. Or if you're writing about your family's history, you could include traditional recipes that have been passed down over time. Maybe certain dishes or foods trigger memories for you, in which case your memoir might comprise a collection of recipes alongside recollections of certain celebrations, family gatherings, romantic experiences, or moments of solitude.

The role of food in your life

Consider the emotions that you and the characters in your life story associate with food. Are certain dishes enjoyed only on joyous occasions? Does a particular recipe remind you of your grandmother before she died? At what times did you eat the meals that you are writing about—in solitude after a loss, at two in the morning with friends, with family after a long day of preparation, or in front of the TV with your mom after she returned from a tiring day at work? What effect does eating have on you: does it calm your nerves or rejuvenate you, or is it an aphrodisiac?

Consider, too, how food and food preparation fit into your culture. Are you a member of the "fast-food nation"? Do you eat healthily to promote an efficient metabolism, or is your diet limited to dishes of a specific nationality or because of your religion? What rituals do you associate with eating—a premeal offering, drinking wine, making conversation, or watching TV?

How important is food to you? Is eating a pleasure or a trial? Like everything else in your life, you will have your own unique, personal relationship with food.

Consider the dishes that have marked special occasions, that became traditions, and the experiences that made them memorable.

VOICES OF THE MASTERS

Nigel Slater, a British chef and food writer, remembers his childhood through food in his memoir *Toast.* The following extract uses marshmallows to recall the period shortly after his mother's death.

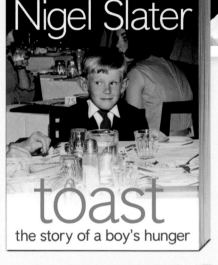

As I snuggled down deep into my bed I saw two white marshmallows on my bedside table. I had never been allowed to eat in bed and when my father came upstairs I asked if they were for me. "Of course they are, I know they're your favorites." They weren't, and he knew it, but I had, in a school essay written shortly before my mother's death, described them as being the nearest food to a kiss. Soft, sweet, tender, pink. True, I had said I didn't like the pink ones but I didn't really mean it. They all tasted the same anyway.

Each night for the next two years I found two, sometimes three, fluffy, sugary marshmallows on my bedside table. It was the goodnight kiss I missed more than anything, more than her hugs, her cuddles, her whispered "Night-night, sleep tight." No Walnut Whip, no Cadbury's Flake, no sugared almond could ever replace that kiss. I'm not sure a marshmallow really came that close.

If you have certain dishes or foodstuff that you associate with specific individuals, use these items to launch your memories—think of how this fare might symbolize your feelings, experience, or relationship.

WRITER'S WORKSHOP

To begin thinking about your relationship to food— what it means to you and the specific memories that are connected to specific foods and meals—here are some memory exercises to get you started.

Bring to mind a dish you're familiar with. Write about:

• The first time you ate it and/or prepared it. Remember to employ the five senses—the presentation or appearance, the aromas or odors, the sensations in your mouth and what the ingredients felt like in your hands, the taste and how it evolved as the food moved along your tongue,

and any sounds produced by the processes of preparing, cooking, and eating.

• A memory associated with the person who prepared or introduced you to this meal.

• Something that happened, or a conversation that took place, when this dish was cooked or consumed.

• The historical and cultural context of this food.

Part Three
Finishing Touches

Narrowing Down Your Audience

By this point you should have produced some kind of first draft—a collection of essays, short stories—or, if yours is a scrapbook project, an organized collection of material and a plan for how you will be laying it out and using text. But before you begin making revisions, it is important to know your audience; this will help you decide which details you should include. The form your project takes gives you a general idea of who you want to read your life story, but now's the time to get specific. When undertaking a project like this, you'll always find that you collect more material than you actually need. Paring it down is one of the challenges of writing your life story.

An audience for your memoirs

Say you're writing your memoirs with a view toward publication: do you think your story will appeal to children, to men and women of all ages, or does its location, subject (your time in the armed forces, for example, or being a mother), or theme (the nihilism of inner-city gang culture, struggling to find your place within society's definitions of beauty) confine it to a more select readership? If your memoirs are concerned with your father's experience of the Holocaust and how this affected you, your readership is not likely to be the same as the one that would enjoy your story about a string of relationships that failed before you reached thirty.

Perhaps you're not hoping for publication, but simply recording your family's story for your children. Read through your work as if speaking aloud to them. Are there sections that seem inappropriate? Are you spilling any family secrets that will do future generations more harm than good if known? At what time in their lives are you expecting your children to read your memoir? Stories of their adventures as toddlers may amuse

them while they are still young but as adult readers, they could find your tone disagreeably sentimental.

Ask yourself if your story is too specific. Do you need to emphasize universal themes within your story in order to broaden your readership and make your project more commercial? If your story is about motherhood, do you need to expand on it so that your memoir might also appeal to men? Maybe not—maybe writing for a female readership will

Knowing your audience is essential—as any marketing executive will tell you. What would your memoir look like if it were published? Do you envision a pink cover and a format that fits easily in a purse, or would your story better suit a handsome hardback, with a smiling photograph of you on the back cover at the golf course?

enable you to include aspects of your story that you feel more comfortable sharing with women than men. Picturing your audience as female doesn't, of course, mean that no men will ever read your book, but it will help you make revisions and add and cut details and scenes so that you wind up with a cohesive story.

An audience for your scrapbook or journal

The same theory applies to your scrapbook or journal: Narrowing down your audience will enable you to decide what details you should include. The travelogue you create for your family will be different from one produced for your friends.

> **Creative projects often develop a life of their own.**

Decide what's more important—your creative outlet or your audience. You don't want to censor yourself or stifle your creativity because you are afraid of offending or isolating somebody you know will read your story. Perhaps now that you've done your research and assembled your stories, your project has taken a different turn from the one you anticipated. Creative projects often develop a life of their own, and though you may have intended to create a scrapbook for your extended family, you might now feel that you want to explore certain issues more intimately in a way that you won't necessarily feel comfortable sharing with your parents.

Be flexible

Think hard about how far you've come with your creative venture and give yourself time to reflect. If, when musing on your experience of collecting memories and ephemera, you feel your story would be better expressed in a different format for a different audience, that's okay. While you were intending to create a journal, your enthusiasm might have catapulted your life story into a project that you feel should be published in order to reach a wider audience. Maybe after reading a few memoirs you no longer feel the need to keep your experiences private. Perhaps you have come across a published story that's similar to your own and now feel inspired to go public. There's nothing wrong with using your first draft to move off into a different format. Consider how much you learned writing your first draft and know that you'll learn at least this much producing a second draft. There are no hard and fast rules: this project is your endeavor and, if and until it goes public, you do not have to answer to anyone but yourself.

You might have started writing for your family but now feel your work deserves a wider audience. Writing is an organic process, and you shouldn't be afraid to follow your creative instincts, even if it means going right back to the beginning.

Getting Feedback from Others

Before you start making revisions, you need to gain some distance from your project. Reviewing your work after a short break will allow you to assess what you've done more objectively. Sharing your work and getting other perspectives can also prove invaluable. Perhaps you have spent months or years deeply engaged in uncovering and assembling your life story. Often, when submerged so deep in a project, it's difficult to take a step back from the experience to view the story as a whole. After all, your mother has always been a mother to you, not a character on a page. When writing a memoir, you relive memories, which often puts you back into the dynamic of your relationship or experience. But when crafting your work, you have to view your memoir for what it is: a story scripted on the page with characters, settings, dialogue, themes, and plot.

Writing workshops

One way to ensure objectivity is to share your story with fellow writers in a writing workshop or class. This will provide you with a safe environment; no one will criticize you or your work just for the sake of criticizing. Workshops are helpful because they teach you how to read and talk about your work. In addition, finding the vocabulary and ability to talk about your classmates' work will help you examine and revise your own.

> **Workshops are helpful because they teach you how to write and talk about your work.**

When the time comes for your work to be placed under scrutiny, it's important to remember that you don't have to take everyone's advice, but you should at least learn how to hear it. Writing is a difficult business and at times requires a thick skin. Remember that when others discuss your writing, they are critiquing what is on the page, not you. Rejection is an inevitable part of the writing process (if you choose to go public with your work), and learning to separate yourself from what you write will not only make you a better editor, it will also increase your ability to survive in the writing business. Even the best authors had their share of rejection letters.

You may find it helpful to air your work at a local group. As writers themselves, your listeners will appreciate the difficulties that you face and may suggest some interesting solutions.

With Mom, 1966

Myself at age 26

With Lucy and Sam, 1972

Finding suitable readers

If you're not ready to take the leap into a workshop, how can you find people to help you? Invite someone you trust to read your work (or review your journal or scrapbook)—maybe your partner or your best friend, but above all, someone capable of constructive criticism, not someone who will praise you when your work is poor or attack you or your writing. Make it clear that you want honest feedback and bear in mind that your reader may not be able to tell you exactly what isn't right with your work.

The best approach is to ask your friend specific questions about your writing. Do the characters seem real? Did she want to keep reading to find out what happened next, or were there moments where she lost interest? Is the language consistent and clear? Can she recognize the protagonist's plight? Did the theme carry through to the end?

At what point you decide to share your work is up to you. When you're ready, be sure to present your reader with a manuscript that is neat and free of typos and basic grammatical errors. If he has negative feedback to offer, you want to ensure that it's in relation to the story and not because he couldn't make sense of your sloppy text. Be prepared for what you might hear, take his constructive criticism on board, and use it to improve your own writing before scripting your next draft.

People have an almost insatiable appetite for stories. Make a character real and your reader will want to know all about her: what her childhood was like, what kind of relationship she had with her mother, what her first job was, how she met her first husband, how she coped with motherhood, and where her life is headed now.

Revision

Many would-be writers never actually pick up a pen because, as avid readers of work they admire, they can't imagine producing anything even half as good. Of course, what they don't appreciate is that the published product is the culmination of umpteen drafts and a great deal of agonizing. The fact is that revision is an essential part of the writing process. If you plan on a future as a writer, it's important that you establish a healthy relationship with this element of your craft from the outset.

Reading through your work

On pages 84–85 we talked about scripting a first draft. At this stage you should write with the simple goal of putting everything down on the page. Do not attempt to edit as you write, and hold nothing back. Better to go off on a tangent now—it might lead you in a new and previously unknown direction, which you may or may not incorporate when you begin to revise.

> ## Do not attempt to edit as you write, and hold nothing back.

You will write many drafts. Before you begin your second draft, read through the first and take notes—either on the manuscript or on a separate page—on how you react to what you read. Do some passages move you more than others? Are you beginning to recognize the presence of a theme? Are there places within the text that should be further developed, opened up, and closely examined in greater detail? Are there places where you feel you have gone into unnecessary detail, which now needs cutting? When you read the work aloud, does the language sound clunky? Make a note of any sentences or paragraphs that require a second or third read for sense (these therefore must be rewritten). How does the dialogue strike you: do the characters come alive on the page? Are you able to tell one character from another? Dialogue is often difficult to get right, and you may want to read it aloud to assess whether or not your characters' speech sounds authentic.

During your second draft you should be concentrating on the finer details—further developing the characters and setting and rewriting any awkward sentences.

What is the story really about? What are your protagonist's goals? What are your story's themes? Make a list of themes as you read and see how, where, and when each shows itself in the text. In later drafts you can add, rewrite, and subtract details and scenes so that each theme is relevant and builds up the picture. Lose any passages in the story that weaken its focus, such as irrelevant incidents or characters or passages that do not reveal anything new or contribute to the plot. Chances are, the more attached you are to a passage or scene, the less it belongs in the text. If you find something that doesn't fit, cut it and save it for another project or a later date. With computers it's just as easy to do this as it is to save every draft, which you should. You might also try isolating elements of your writing for closer examination—dialogue, setting, characters, plot, and so on—to help determine how well each works.

Revision takes time, and if you've been sitting in front of your manuscript for a while without making progress, take a break. While it's important to be disciplined, you shouldn't be too hard on yourself. Those hours spent contemplating in front of your computer screen are a part of the process, as is the time in your car, online, and before sleep that you spend thinking about your story. Though they may seem unproductive, those moments where you sit and think are actually an integral part of your work.

Restructuring

If you've read through your first draft and feel like nothing works, put your writing aside for a while, then read it again. If still nothing seems right, perhaps you need to restructure your story. Break your story down into scenes. Put a brief description of each scene on a note card with the relevant page number, and then number the cards in the order in which they appear. You can then pin your cards

onto a large bulletin board and restructure your story by moving them around. Once you've found a sequence—a storyboard—that works, you can return to the computer and cut and paste the scenes into their new order. Working with cards in this way is far easier than literally cutting and pasting the pages of your manuscript as they lay strewn across the floor of your living room.

If you're failing to make headway on screen, try printing out your work and reading it aloud. Alternatively, call it a day and, with luck, your subconscious will come up with a solution while you are asleep.

When you can read your manuscript without encountering errors, you're done.

Proofreading

Once you have a version you are pleased with, run through your manuscript looking for errors in grammar, punctuation, and spelling. This should be the final process in your edit. When you can read your manuscript without encountering errors, you're done. Be careful not to overwork your piece—you run the risk of disrupting the organic pacing of your story or of altering the natural sound of your voice. You do not want your narrative or voice to become stiff or sound forced. Don't look for something to correct simply because you can't bear the thought of completing your project.

Assessing Your Achievement

As you near the final stage of your project, take a moment to reflect upon your journey. Did you achieve all that you set out to do? If you suspect that you have fallen short of the expectations you established before starting your project and you still feel these expectations deserve to be met, you can now take the opportunity to reassess and make changes.

Reassessing your work

Before you take the time to reassess your life story project, it's best to put it aside for a while. With all this time spent so closely involved and engaged, it's important to first take a step back so that you might gain a bit of distance from the project before you begin to critically examine just where you've been and whether your journey has produced the result you set out to achieve.

After both you and your work have been given room to breathe reread your project with an objective eye. If you intended to tell a complete story, does your project accomplish this? If your intention was to paint a picture of a family history, convey the trials and tribulations of a personal experience, share a triumph, better understand your subject, solve a mystery, or document a life-changing period or event, ask yourself if the completed project succeeds in achieving this.

When reassessing your work, ask yourself if you've pushed yourself far or hard enough. Were your initial goals too easily obtained, or do you see any places where you could open up and explore or reveal more? Reconsider your intentions. When first beginning a project, your unfamiliarity with the process might lead you to set your goals short. Now that you're more familiar with what you can achieve, do you think you can now set the bar a little higher to make your project more interesting or more suited to the message you'd hoped to convey?

Consider the audience for whom you've created your life-story project. Is the material you've presented readily available? Are all questions raised eventually answered? Will your intended readership be able to picture, feel, and experience the life you wrote about? Do your characters come across as you intended? While you want the reader to be able to imagine the extremes, you also want to make sure that you, as a writer, achieved a sense of balance that is maintained throughout your journal, scrapbook, or manuscript.

It's important to leave a period between writing your initial draft and reading it through to assess it. Coming back to it, after even a short period of time, will help you see your work more objectively.

WRITER'S WORKSHOP

Reviewing your journey It's important to look back on the months—or years—you spent writing your memoir. At this point you should feel a sense of accomplishment. Ask yourself:

• What were your goals when you started out?

• Were you using your project to reach out to certain individuals in order to share certain aspects of your life?

• What did you hope to communicate to these individuals and how did you expect it to change your relationship?

• How has the experience of writing changed you?

• What did you learn? Is any of this a surprise?

• Did you learn what you expected about the family you researched or the individuals you incorporated into your life story?

• Did any of the encounters you experienced through your research affect the ways in which you view or live your life?

• Perhaps your project was meant to help you recover from a relationship or an event, to better understand yourself or an experience, to forgive, or to be able to move on and forget.

• Do you have a sense of closure as you near the end of your project, or did you discover new avenues that need to be explored? (If you answered yes to the latter question, be sure to record your feelings and ideas.)

• How different is your first draft from what you'd expected?

• What did you learn in the process, and did you manage to incorporate this knowledge into your story?

• Did your protagonist achieve something other than what you'd expected?

• Did any surprising themes appear?

• Does what you've written pose any unanswered questions? If so, reexamine the focus of your story to ensure that every scene, every character, and every subtheme reveals something new to the reader and comes together to paint a picture in its entirety.

• Does your story include any characters who exit shortly after they appear, leaving the reader dissatisfied?

• Is every aspect of your project as developed as it could be? (Ask yourself this question for every scene, every setting, every theme, and every detail. Be sure that you are satisfied with each so that you can exit this phase of your life story with a sense of closure.)

The process of writing your life story can be an emotionally demanding experience. Now that it is over, do you feel a sense of catharsis, as though a burden has been lifted from you? Or do you feel there is still more to be said?

Legal Issues

Perhaps somewhere in your life story you've decided you want to include the work of others, whether it's your aunt May, Bob Dylan, or J. D. Salinger, because she or he has influenced your life or your story, or because her or his work serves as a backdrop to a scene. Maybe you want to include your grandmother's recipe in a scrapbook, reproduce an interview, include song lyrics, or feature extracts from someone's blog (Internet diary).

Citing your sources

The medium in which you choose to include the work of another will determine the steps you need to take in order to ensure that your reproductions are honest and legal. As long as your work is not intended for a public audience, you don't need to concern yourself with copyright issues. However, you should still give credit where credit is due, by citing the source in parentheses in the text, in a footnote, or in a separate note to the reader. In addition, if you're quoting a family member from an interview, you owe it to the speaker to properly record his or her words.

> You owe it to the speaker to get his or her words right

Check what you've written against your transcript of the interview. Finally, you have a contract with the reader to tell the truth. This principle applies even if your intended readers are your children, who will later read about their lives in the scrapbook, journal, or memoir you've created for them.

My back pages

Thursday, May 18

We went to see Bob Dylan in concert tonight and it sent me right back to my record collection and my copy of Blonde on Blonde which I haven't played in many, many years. And do you know what - it sounded as fresh and vital as it did way back in the mists of time when the word was younger and so was I. A lot has happened since then but I don't think my enjoyment of his music has changed one jot. I had no idea then how much he would still mean to me some 30 years later. I've changed a lot but his music is timeless.

Monday, May 22

Lots of things seem to mark the passage of the years but nothing so much as seeing your children growing up. One minute they are clinging to your trouser leg and looking up at you the next they are towering over you. It's difficult to see the link between the little child and the young adult who blossoms before your eyes.

About me

Name:
Kevin
Where I live:
Washington

Family
My Wife:
Pat
My Kids:
Chloe
Julia

Other stuff
Interests:
Music
Family history
Jogging
Sailing
Reading
Heroes:
Salinger
Dylan

If "Blowin' in the Wind" changed your perspective on life, it makes sense to include the lyrics in your memoir. Just remember that Dylan not you, owns those words.

WRITER'S WORKSHOP

Writing for publication When writing for publication, you must pay attention to the rules regarding libel and copyright. Libel is defined by *Webster's Dictionary* as "defamation of a person by written or representational means." This means that you need to be circumspect about the secrets you reveal and how you depict other people in your stories in order to avoid offending someone unduly or being sued. Different countries have different libel practices and rules, and the publisher who takes on your work should be able to advise you about possible libel issues.

According to the U.S. Copyright Office's website (www.copyright.gov/), all written text is considered in copyright from the moment it is written. For the most part, a writer's work remains in copyright for seventy years after death, but there may be exceptions. What should you do if you found your grandmother's letters a few years after she died and want to include excerpts in your memoir? Copyright is the right of the author or the author's heirs or assignees (not of the person who possesses the physical work), so you need to make sure that you own the work by will or by inheritance.

What should you do if you want to reproduce a paragraph of text, a poem, or a song in your work? Copyright laws vary from country to country and from state to state. In general, it is best to seek legal advice on the situation in your country or area if you have any doubts concerning the copyright of a particular work. According to the U.S. Copyright Office, "Under the fair use doctrine of the U.S. copyright statute, it is permissible to use limited portions of a work including quotes, for purposes such as commentary, criticism, news reporting, and scholarly reports. There are no legal rules permitting the use of a specific number of

words, a certain number of musical notes, or percentage of a work. Whether a particular use qualifies as fair use depends on all the circumstances." For this reason, when reproducing work that has already been published—and particularly in the case of even a single line from a song or poem—it is advisable to seek permission from the copyright holder. Sometimes fees will then have to be paid to the rightful owner of the images, songs, or text.

The UK Copyright Service (copyrightservice.co.uk) offers fact sheets and answers to common copyright questions, as well as a copyright registration service. In Australasia, try the Copyright Agency Limited (www.copyright.com.au/home.htm) in Australia, and the Copyright Council of New Zealand (www.copyright.org.nz/).

Your copyright questions can be answered via many sites on the Internet. Remember, laws vary from country to country and state to state.

Designing Your Book

How you present your life story should reveal something about you, whether it's a reflection of your taste or representative of your personality. The way you package your work should also complement your purpose and the story you are telling (unless you are writing for publication; see pages 180–181). The options are numerous: you can arrange your pictures and text in a book you've made from scratch or from a kit, alter an existing book, or buy a blank one that you simply fill in.

Making a book from scratch

Do you want to design your own journal or scrapbook? This is quite a complex venture that entails folding the paper into sections (with the paper grain going in the right direction), sewing, gluing, or securing the spine in some way, and then making a cover for it. Bookmaking publications, such as *Cover to Cover: Creative Techniques for Making Beautiful Books, Journals, and Albums* by Shereen LaPlantz and the more technically advanced *Penland Book of Homemade Books: Master Classes in Bookmaking Techniques,* published by Lark, guide you through the bookmaking process. You can also research local bookbinding classes and additional reading on the subject.

Making a book from a kit

If you want to make a book, but not from scratch, you can choose from many readily available album kits. Try the Paper Source, which sells a range of photo album kits with either black or white pages, as well as materials and tools for bookbinding, including book boards (the hard covers of a book) and text blocks (the actual pages containing the content of the book: illustrations and text), which you can combine to make your own books. Other useful sites are Scrapbook Gifts

(www.scrapbookgifts.com), which has a wide selection of scrapbook and journal kits and offers a selection of supplies; Craft Products Australia (www.craftonline.com.au/shopping/c-albums. asp), for scrapbooks and albums with different types of cover; and Scrapbooking Castle (www. scrapbookingcastle.co.uk/store) for album kits and a variety of papers.

Making a book requires patience and skill. The reward is that, free from the constraints of commercial publishing, you can use the specialist tools and materials available to create a work of art that perfectly complements your story.

Altering an existing book

If you have a favorite novel or picture book that you feel represents who you are, you can alter it to make it your journal or scrapbook by covering the text with pages of your own or by incorporating your own images and text into the existing ones. A few books explore this unusual technique, including *Altered Book Collage* by Barbara Matthiessen and *The Complete Guide to Altered Imagery: Mixed Media Techniques for Collage, Altered Books, Artist Journals, and More* by Karen Michel.

> If you find that your choices are limited, you can extend your search online.

Buying a ready-made book

If you want to purchase a journal, start with a visit to your local art-supply store. You may want blank rather than lined pages, since blank pages allow you to include images or drawings without visual interference. If you find that your choices are limited, you can extend your search online. Websites such as www.journalbooks.com/main/index.php let you create your own custom design, or allow you to choose among a number of styles, including leather or aluminum bound.

When it comes to scrapbooks, you can choose from expandable albums (to which you can add or subtract your own pages), post-bound albums (which are bound with a set of screws), strap-hinge albums (which are bound with a single strap), spiral-bound, and leather-bound albums (which have front and back covers and pages that are permanently bound together). Whatever style you choose, make sure the book is constructed with materials that won't harm your ephemera. Acid or petroleum-based products could eventually destroy your scrapbook contents, so look for products that are labeled "acid-free," "photo-safe," or "archival quality."

When selecting a readymade scrapbook, consider your readership. If your project is meant for all the family to enjoy, choose materials that will withstand grubby fingers and repeated reading.

Adding Captions

If you are including images in your project, you need to think about what kind of accompanying text will best convey your message. Inspirational quotations, poems, songs, story excerpts, interviews, and journal excerpts are all options—each will establish a different tone throughout.

Deciding on a style

What kind of text do you want to include with your image? You might begin by free-writing about it to see what comes up. Perhaps through one of the exercises in this book, you've created text that refers to the person, place, situation, or time referred to in the image. Maybe you've interviewed someone and have an excerpt that could accompany a picture. Alternatively, if you've kept a daily journal, perhaps you have entries from the time when the photograph was taken.

When you've amassed as much written material as you can, in relation or in response to a particular image, read what you have and choose the text you like. If one passage doesn't stand out, combine and edit the text with a new response to your material.

Photos come to life when accompanied by a stimulating caption. If your own words can't suffice, perhaps a song or poem will do. A caption can be as long or as short and punchy as you like.

"She ran calling Wildfire."

Wildfire

She comes down from Yellow Mountain
On a dark, flat land she rides
On a pony she named Wildfire
With a whirlwind by her side

On a cold Nebraska night...

She ran calling Wildfire...

We'll be riding Wildfire

On Wildfire we're gonna ride
Gonna leave sodbustin' behind
Get these hard times right our of our minds
Riding Wildfire"

Larry Cansler and Michael Martin Murphy

Providing a wider context

If you're interested in incorporating published works in your captions, you might want to choose a favorite book, song, or poem that dates from the time of the photograph to provide context for the reader. Did you identify with a character in a novel when you were 16? You could select an extract from that novel and run it alongside a picture of yourself at that age.

Interested in historical context? You could research and write a caption about the time in which your photograph was taken, providing the reader with more insight into the period. If you plan to include documents, such as marriage or death certificates or property deeds, you could write about the document, interview a relative who lived at that time, or visit the place that pertains to the records (a house of worship or temple, cemetery, or piece of real estate) and summarize your findings in the caption.

Engaging your reader

Once you've rewritten your caption text a few times and are sure it's complete, you need to think about presentation. You could handwrite your entries (after practicing to ensure a steady hand), which lends a personal touch to the presentation. You can find many tools to help you style your writing (see page 169). You could also script your entries on a computer and experiment with different fonts. If you choose this option, you can more easily preserve, edit, and organize your various drafts. Or for short passages, you could use rubber stamps (choose ones with lines).

Whatever you do, don't shy away from writing. In some places a short, punchy caption may be appropriate, but if you have a story to tell, don't be afraid to use an extended caption or two to tell it. These passages will deepen the reader's engagement with your life story.

of his mother
Marker thin

of his mother
Giddyup

of his mother
Bickham script

of his mother
Caflish script

of his mother
Zapfino

The memory of his mother on her bicycle does not leave him. She pedals away up Poplar Avenue, escaping from him, escaping towards her own desire. He does not want her to go. He does not want her to have a desire of her own. He wants her always to be in the house, waiting for him when he comes home.

Boyhood, J. M. Coetzee

Each typeface communicates its own mood: an italic script with elaborate flourishes could suggest a bygone era, for example. Be sure your captions are legible. With so many scripts available, it's tempting to mix and match, but the overall effect will be messy.

Travelogues

Traveling almost always produces interesting stories. Let's say you've chosen a particular journey or a series of trips as the subject of your life story. Any one of the three mediums—journal, scrapbook, or memoir—is an excellent place to explore travel as your theme.

Incorporating a theme

Whether you plan to use journal entries and letters, write a chronological memoir or produce a series of short stories or essays based on specific subjects, such as food, trains, monuments, wildlife, language, or place, but don't get carried away with writing about the place and forget about the need for character, dialogue, plot, theme, detail, and voice.

Like any other memoir, your story needs a protagonist who embarks on a journey—your reader shouldn't be simply moved from one location to another. How does your protagonist change over the course of your travel story? What does she learn? Remember that travel books and encyclopedias cover the facts; your experience can be far more subjective.

Ever had a friend bore you with their vacation snaps? No matter how stunning your collection of images, a travelogue needs to tell a good story, and not necessarily one that starts on day one and ends with your flight home.

Local wildlife

Playful children

A place of serenity

WRITER'S WORKSHOP

Reading travelogues can help you develop a structure for your stories and give you ideas of what to look for in a written travel account. Here are some inspiring suggestions to get you started:

Lost Japan by Alex Kerr.

Love and War in the Apennines by Eric Newby.

A Year in Provence by Peter Mayle.

Driving over Lemons: An Optimist in Andalucía by Chris Stewart.

Lonely Planet travel literature series.

Collections of travel essays, such as:

The Best Women's Travel Writing 2005, edited by Lucy McCauley.

Voyage of the Beagle: Selected Writings of Charles Darwin, edited by Michael Kerrigan.

Italian Tours: Travel Essays by Henry James, edited by John Auchard.

D. H. Lawrence, Travel and Cultural Difference by Neil Roberts.

Waugh Abroad: Collected Travel Writing, introduced by Nicholas Shakespeare.

Writing East: The "Travels" of Sir John Mandeville by Iain M. Higgins.

Other Routes: African and Asian Travel Writings from before 1900, edited by Justin D. Edwards.

VOICES OF THE MASTERS

How are you planning to structure the story of your journey—by place, by the individuals you met, by adventure, or by food? If you don't have a collection of photographs for your project, look for postcards, stock photographs, magazine articles, and paintings that complement your story. You might even make a collage integrating the various components that formed the emotional, cultural, physical, or natural experience of your trip. Once you have gathered your collection of photographs, tickets, postcards, product labels, newspaper and magazine clippings, menus, drawings, and so on, revisit the previous spread (pages 152–153) and start to picture how you should integrate your ephemera with text.

Isak Dinesen (the pen name of Baroness Karen Blixen) wrote *Out of Africa,* which described the years she spent managing a coffee plantation in Kenya from 1914 to 1941. Her book is divided into five sections, each of which contains from four to thirty-two passages, with titles including "The Somali Women," "The Eclipse of the Moon," and "Fellow-Travelers." This structure enables her to move around from topic to topic, varying the length of each passage as necessary. The following excerpt comes from the section entitled "The Iguana."

> *Once I shot an Iguana. I thought that I should be able to make some pretty things from his skin. A strange thing happened then, that I have never afterwards forgotten. As I went up to him, where he was lying dead upon his stone, and actually while I was walking the few steps, he faded and grew pale, all color died out of him as in one long sigh, and by the time that I touched him he was gray and dull like a lump of concrete. It was the live impetuous blood pulsating within the animal, which had radiated out all that glow and splendor. Now that the flame was put out, and the soul had flown, the Iguana was as dead as a sandbag.*

You may be creating a life story that is mostly pictorial, but you can still script a collection of stunning passages, such as the one above, to enhance your ephemera and photographs.

Family Trees

If you've done a lot of genealogical research for your scrapbook, journal, or memoir, you may want to create a family tree as a visual addition to your life story. You can, of course, chart your family's names using simple lines to connect the individuals, but why not produce something unique? A family tree as a piece of art makes a great cover for a family scrapbook. You could also use one to suggest a structure or layout for your project by beginning with the information you discovered on the founders of your family and continuing with the members that followed. If you plan to incorporate several generations into your life story, including a tree will also prove a useful aid for the reader.

Choosing your visual

If you're not artistically inclined, take a photograph of a tree and insert your family's names on the branches. Alternatively, create a collage of a tree, inserting photographs of family members in place of fruit. There are also websites that sell family tree kits (try www.family-trees.tripod.com) and companies that will create a personalized tree for you (see www.afamilyconnection.com). Browse books and the Internet for other examples that will give you inspiration.

> Take a photograph of a tree and insert your family's names on the branches.

Artist Elaine Adler creates personalized family trees in Hebrew and English, incorporating calligraphy, calligraphic design, and trees (see www. elaineadler.com/FamilyTrees_Pages/frameset_ FamilyTrees.html). The family tree from her website depicted at right shows how the family members are related and it reveals something personal about each individual. It also shows two trees joined together by branches that represent the union of the married couple.

Holly Monroe, a calligrapher, exhibits different types of family trees on her website (www.hollymonroe.com/ portfolio/familytrees/ familytrees.html). In one sample she includes lettering within the branches of the tree and roots, making the family names form the actual tree instead of having the tree support family names. In another, she adds another dimension by using photographs.

Incorporating a visual is useful. Here, the branches reveal photographs rather than just the names of the family members.

This tree, created by Elaine Adler, was commissioned as a gift from three children to their parents. Each family member is represented by a decorative icon: a theatrical mask for the comedian of the family, and, moving up the generations, a horse-drawn cart for a peddler.

Playing with the traditional tree format, calligrapher Holly Monroe illustrates the joining together of two families in marriage. The branches extend outward to place the individuals in a wider context of community than would a more formal representation.

Altered Art

Altered art makes use of objects that originally held esthetic value of their own, such as maps, photographs, stamps, banknotes, books, magazines, documents, tickets, and postcards. You might display these objects individually on the page, in pairs, or as a visual collection. Even if you haven't collected much, there's a lot you can find by rummaging through your family's photograph albums, going to flea markets, searching at antique shops, and even looking online. Altered art is an accessible medium, using ephemera that are easy to come by and should be tried if you're interested in creative expression.

Presenting your collections

Perhaps you have a collection of menus from special occasions (birthday dinners or weddings), maps from your travels, or photographs. In this case the items you choose to combine as altered art will hint at the original stories behind the events at which they were collected. They could also suggest your thoughts or feelings in reaction to them or even the end result of the event. You can also assemble photographs of family and friends with other ephemera to reveal something about their character or experience to the viewer. A collection of matchbox packaging from India, for instance, might suggest the excitement of travel to far-flung places, stepping back into a past era, or the vibrant colors associated with Indian life.

Nick Bantock's *Urgent 2nd Class: Creating Curious Collage, Dubious Documents, and Other Art from Ephemera* offers many examples of altered

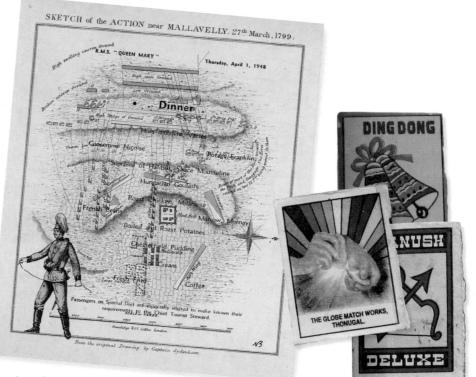

art, including how to make "Faux Mail" and "Dubious Documents," and various ways to use rubber stamps, postcards, photocopies, money, and engravings. Above is a sample taken from his chapter on "maps."

Old tickets, menus, postcards, maps, and stamps can all be pasted into your scrapbook to help tell your life story.

A stamp on the surface of an image can lend it an archival quality, and anchor it in time and place.

Also in *Urgent 2nd Class*, Bantock cuts and combines banknotes from other time periods and countries. It's a compelling way to display the monies you've collected on your trips. In his chapter on photographs, he explains the process of phototransfer alongside a sample image. It is not advisable to paste old original photographs into your journal or scrapbook (for the sake of preservation), and phototransfer is an excellent way to display such imagery.

WRITER'S WORKSHOP

Digital Collage If you're creating a digital scrapbook, you can still make use of the various ephemera and photographs collected, to help illustrate your life story. You might choose to scan your images and ephemera, or use digital photographs of your tickets, stamps, and labels. You can then use any of the numerous software programs (see page 172) to download, cut, overlap, and paste your images on screen.

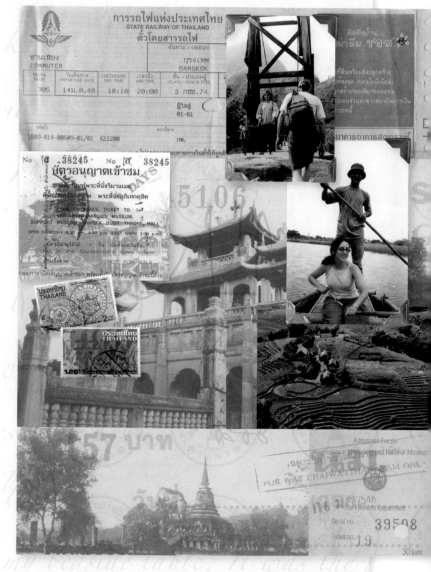

Photographs and Photography

With the high-quality cameras and equipment available these days, you don't have to be a professional to achieve good results. Rather than drawing on existing photographs, you may want to put together a collection especially for your project. If so, one of the first decisions you need to make is whether you want your final product to be hard copy or a digital presentation; this will determine whether you shoot digital photographs or use a 35-mm camera. (Of course, you can always scan your scrapbook and make it digital or print out a copy of your digital production; see pages 172–175.) You also need to choose between color or black and white—although you may opt to use a mixture of both.

Choosing the best photographs

If you already have a collection of photographs, whether they're your grandmother's or your own, you need to sort through and select what you want to include. Your choices may be guided by your writing, which means choosing photographs that best illustrate your text. If you used images to inspire your writing, you will probably want to include these, or you might opt to tell one story with text while offering another perspective through your selected imagery.

If you need one picture of your brother as a child and have many to choose from, look for the photograph that best captures his personality at the time. Also look at how the photographs are composed. Does one strike you as more visually

Black-and-white photographs evoke a sense of distance and time past, whereas color images seem to reflect the world as we see it now, thus grabbing us with their immediacy. Choose the effect that best suits your project.

pleasing or stimulating than another? Composition affects how your eye moves around the image. Where does your eye begin and how does it move around the photograph? If you find that your eye is led around the entire frame, then chances are you have a well-composed photograph.

> **Begin by visually isolating the image you wish to capture.**

Taking the best photographs

Whether you use digital or print film, the way in which you photograph is basically the same. Begin by visually isolating the image you wish to capture, whether it's a person or a group of people, a landscape, an action, or an interior. Ask yourself why this image is relevant to your story. What new information does the photograph provide? Is this shot the best way to convey it? You don't need to have the answers to these questions the moment you decide to shoot (photography is often a spontaneous medium), but you should apply these questions when deciding which pictures you choose to include.

Look at the scene. How much light is there and where is it coming from? Can you get away with not using a flash? Some lights and light angles are more flattering than others. Lighting an individual from above—especially with sunlight—is generally not a flattering approach. It creates shadows in inappropriate places, so try to make use of natural light that falls on your subject from an angle (early day or evening sunlight is best; avoid noon). Only use flash if you know how to use it off the camera and how to adjust the exposures. Artificial light generally flattens the subject and either washes it out (overexposes certain areas) or illuminates all areas of the frame equally, which generally results in a visually unappealing or inaccurate depiction.

WRITER'S WORKSHOP

One advantage of digital photography is that you can take as many photographs as you want without "wasting film." Your best pictures are likely to be the ones you take when your subject has gotten bored of posing and forgotten the camera is there.

Portraits When photographing people, try to focus more on capturing moments rather than posing your subjects. People naturally wear a wide range of expressions but rarely the ones they put on when posing for a photograph. The following tips will help you take portraits that communicate something more about the people in the frame than simply what they look like.

- Try to capture people in their elements. Where does your subject shine—at athletic competitions, when relaxed, alone, or with others, when laughing, concentrating, or on an adventure?

- Think of ways in which you might engage your subject. Anyone can snap a picture of an individual smiling for a photograph, but how might your relationship with your sitter affect your portrayal of him?

- Experiment by having your subject look into and away from the lens. Photograph her standing up, sitting down, or in repose. How can you best capture the essence of her being?

- Photograph your subject in a range of different environments that you feel say something about her.

- Whatever the background, be careful how you arrange your sitter in front of it. Look out for strange objects, such as tree branches or light poles that might seem to be coming out of her head.

Showing the passing of time

Perhaps you want to document how people change. Beginning in 1975, Nicholas Nixon, an American photographer, used an 8 x 10-inch camera to photograph his wife and her three sisters. Every year, the Brown sisters sat or stood in the same order, looked into the camera, and were caught in black and white, documented as they aged. In a variety of seasons and scenes, the sisters posed together, revealing something about themselves, their relationships, and their frailty as they changed from adolescents to middle-aged women. The series spans 1975 to 1987 and is featured in Nixon's book *Pictures of People*.

Each photograph shows how the sisters have changed. While their positions within the frame are consistent (as is the photographer's perspective), their dress, hair, bodies, and skin are not. The viewer, who is not a family member and so views the shots objectively, is left to imagine the evolution these women have undergone as they have grown and changed.

Exploring every angle

When writing, you examine each character thoroughly (his appearance, gestures, voice, relationships, actions, and possible conflicts). When taking photographs, you should do the

You can't tell the whole story with a single image. Explore a scene from as many angles as you can to suggest the experience of the different characters within it. Complement your close-ups by pulling back occasionally to show "the big picture."

Making sandcastles

Playing in the rock pools

same. What is the context of the scene you are hoping to capture? If your subject is a building, are there any details you'd like to capture close up, in addition to shooting the structure as a whole? How does this structure fit within its environment? What is its context? Should you include people? What are the angles from which you should shoot—from above (avoid looking down at children; it is best to show a child within his own realm rather than as perceived from an adult perspective), at eye level, at a distance, close up, or from below? If you're photographing something from an unavoidable distance, such as wildlife, use a telephoto or zoom lens for a more immediate image.

Improving your skills

The only way to improve your photographer's eye is to look at photographs and to photograph more. Just as you carry around your pocket notebook to capture soundbites and thoughts, you should carry your camera; you never know what you might come across. Visit your local bookstore or library and spend an afternoon looking at photography books. What makes these professional images different from yours? Pull out your albums and pick out the images that you think work best. Try writing about your viewing experience and applying what you learn the next time you select a photograph or raise the camera to your eye.

Looking for crabs

Waiting for the waves

Photo Display

With your collection of photographs at hand, old and new, you'll need to consider how to display these images on the page. There are many ways to present photographs—black-and-white images with white borders held in place with black mounting corners on a black page, or color snapshots mounted and framed with patterned fabrics. How you present your pictures will help determine the tone of your scrapbook or journal.

Copying the originals

Never alter or adhere an original photograph without duplicating it first. One-of-a-kind images, such as old photographs without negatives, should be scanned or copied before being included in your book, and even then the original should not be glued to the page.

> Never alter or adhere an original photograph without duplicating it first.

Cropping

It's preferable to crop when taking your photograph—to compose the image in your viewfinder before you release the shutter—but you may need to crop after the picture has been taken. In addition, you may choose to use cropping as an element of your design.

When should you crop an image? Perhaps your photograph is too large to fit on the page or your principal subject constitutes only a small portion of the frame and you would like to isolate and enhance its presence.

Cropping allows you to cut out any distracting or unwanted elements and to place your subject center stage. If you're not sure how a crop will look, use a makeshift cardboard frame and experiment by laying it over the image.

Cropping tools

Scissors with sharp, fine points are good for detail-oriented work, such as cutting silhouettes from photographs.

Craft knives (handles with replaceable blades) allow you to cut clean, straight lines with the aid of a ruler or T-square.

Shape cutters can either work like cookie cutters, with edges sharp enough to cut through paper and cardstock, or as templates that you can trace onto your photographs before cutting with scissors or a craft knife. You can also find other handheld tools, such as compass cutters, which cut circles with a blade that pivots around a central spike.

Punches allow you to cut shapes directly into your photographs and come in a variety of sizes and shapes.

Using mats

If you choose to silhouette an image by cutting along the edges of your subject, you might opt to ground its floating appearance by using a mat. Usually 1/8 to 1/4-inch larger than the photograph itself, the mat generally follows the shape of the photograph that it is backing and comes in a wide range of colors. However, you don't have to silhouette your photographs in order to mat them. You might choose to spruce up your display by "framing" your images with mats in colors chosen to complement each photograph. In this case the mat can be anywhere from 1/4 inch to 1 inch larger than the photograph itself. When the picture is adhered to the mat, it appears framed.

WRITER'S WORKSHOP

Framing If you want to actually frame your pictures, you can make use of overlays, which are precut pieces of cardstock with a single window (or more than one window) cut out of the board. This enables you to simply lay the cardstock over the pictures you wish to crop or frame. If you prefer more unusually sized and shaped windows, you can cut your own with a craft knife and ruler or T-square.

Mounting When mounting your photographs, the less adhesive you use, the better. You should always have the opportunity to remove the picture from the page. There are many mounting options to choose from, depending on your desired effect—mounting corners, photo pockets, and adhesive dots. Whatever your method, ensure that your papers, boards, tapes, and glues are acid-free or of archival quality to avoid contaminating your photographs and ephemera and thereby causing deterioration.

Making an oval frame

Use a die-cut and craft knife, or a specialist oval cutter to cut an oval out of white card. Practice first to ensure your oval will frame your image effectively.

If the photograph is the same size as the frame, use mounting corners to fix the two together. Otherwise place the photograph between the frame and a piece of cardboard and glue the pieces of card together to hold the photograph in place.

Designing the Page

What style are you trying to achieve? Do you envision something old-fashioned with sepia prints, something more poplike and colorful, or maybe a combination of the two? The style will set the overall tone of the story and is as important as the text.

Creating harmony

The items you choose to include will play a large part in determining your book's style, so give some thought to how your pieces come together. What colors do you plan to use on each page? Do they complement each other? Will many of your photographs be cut into different shapes, or are they the standard-size black-and-white photos with white borders? What combinations of styles work well together? Which don't? How does the shade and texture (or pattern) of the paper in your scrapbook suit the items you wish to include? Whether you decide to use frames and borders, block stamps for text, or to illustrate your pages, your materials should harmonize with each other. Consider all the visual elements—color schemes, patterns, textures, shapes, and text—as you assemble each page.

Move your material around the page to see which combinations are most effective. Does each element contribute to the page as a whole? Does the reader know where to look first?

Louise aged 8 with her school friends

Portraits of Grandma

It is a good idea to make a rough plan of each page before securing all the separate elements in place.

Producing a rough draft

Before you begin gluing down your ephemera, construct a rough or first draft. This may be in the form of sketches that illustrate your page designs, or you could go through your scrapbook and pencil in each piece of ephemera. Consider the order of your pages. Remember, you are still telling a story; think about how your pages relate to each other. Is it wise to follow a page on your sister as a kid with a page on your travels? What is your narrative? Make sure that the pages come together to create a whole.

Make a note of how your eye travels around the page. Does it flow smoothly from one item to another or does it jump haphazardly? Try grounding the page by placing heavier or larger objects near the bottom and lighter objects near the top.

Layering can be used to create depth on the page. Experiment with layering photographs or frames, shapes or blocks of color, and letters. You can even use raised adhesive dots to add dimension or depth to the page.

WRITER'S WORKSHOP

Decorative pages Once you've decided upon a visual theme, keep it consistent. If you're interested in framing your images, then do so throughout your book. Shop for a selection of fabrics that complement each other and don't clash. You will want to be able to mix and match your solids and patterns, which will provide variety from page to page. You can also use different fabrics or papers to create a layered-frame look. Choose two or three patterns or solids (or mix and match) that complement each other and the image you're aiming to frame.

Making a decorative page

Measure and cut each sheet so that one is nearly a half of an inch larger than the other, on all sides.

Glue the layers atop each other, before attaching the final product onto your scrapbook page. You might also frame your captions to keep the presentation consistent and neat.

WRITER'S WORKSHOP

Tools and equipment Paper comes in a wide variety of colors, patterns, and prints, including metallic papers and translucent vellums. You can use paper not only to create borders and frames, but also as decorative shapes and letters. Try color blocking, which uses squares and rectangles to create a mosaic-like appearance on the page; paper folding, which is similar to origami; crumpling (after dampening, the paper will have a leathery look); and paper weaving. You can find numerous books and websites that highlight some of these techniques.

Paper-cutting dies are like cookie cutters for paper and come in a variety of shapes and sizes, from suns and flowers to letters and holiday-specific designs. They can be bought in packages of precut die-cuts (which, if laser cut, can be quite intricately designed) or used with die-cutting machines. Some companies have thousands of dies to choose from. These shapes can be used for lettering, framing (by placing a photo in the middle of the die-cut), layering to produce a shadow effect, or to create designs. You can also decorate your die-cuts with chalks, inks, glitters, and paints.

Punches are an easier way to create shapes from paper: they're smaller and more portable, but not interchangeable. Like die-cuts, they come in a variety of shapes and sizes, but you can decorate, frame, layer, and create borders with just circles and squares. Remember to create your layout first, moving the pieces and images around until you are satisfied with the composition, before you begin gluing anything down.

Templates are a good option if die-cuts seem too complicated or involved. Use them to trace shapes onto photographs or paper before cutting along the edges of your drawn line. Then use the resulting shapes just as you would use those created by punches or die-cuts.

Scissors come in a variety of sizes and blades. Those with smaller blades are better for more detail-oriented work; some have decorative edges that create patterns as you cut, which can be used for borders, pages, and frames. Circle scissors (which have a clear view-rotating disk to enable you to see what you are cutting, and a pen blade) can be used to create up to 125 different circle sizes (but use a mat underneath to protect your table surface).

rubber stamps

buttons and beads

Rubber stamps can be used to decorate, to letter or number, or to create tags on which you can identify images or script short journal excerpts. You can also use a variety of stencils for the same purpose.

Pens come in a vast range, so give ample consideration to the tools you'll use to script your text. Whether you're writing long stories, journal excerpts, or simply captions, you need to consider not only your colors but also the type of inks you will use, the texture of the pen's tip, and the size of its point. Obviously, a finer-tipped pen is required for journaling so that your text can be read easily. Markers, colored pencils, and chalks are useful for titling, highlighting, or outlining. If you're interested in calligraphy, you might want to use it to enhance your journal or scrapbook—just make sure you are familiar with the art. There are numerous lettering kits—which include inks, instructional booklets, and pen nibs—on the market to help you learn the craft,.

Scrapbook accessories If you're not satisfied with creating layouts using only photographs and text, ephemera (including collage), and a few frames and shapes, you can peruse the world of scrapbook accessories—but be careful not to overuse these or you'll create a cluttered look. Scrapbook accessories include stickers (which come in a variety of materials), beads, buttons, sequins, fabrics, wooden items, fibers, and tags.

Developing your scrapbooking skills

The ideas mentioned here will get you started on your scrapbook. Organize your material into pages and play around with the layouts. If the medium captures your imagination, look into other sources that provide additional tips and support.

fiber-tipped pens

calligraphy pen and nibs

Going Digital

If you haven't already made the move from print cameras to digital, you might now consider the transition, if only for the ease of storing, organizing, and printing photographs for your journal or scrapbook. Digital cameras not only save money with their reusable compact flashcards (or other digital storage device) instead of film but also allow you to view your pictures immediately and print only the images you choose. The camera's ability to delete unwanted images, along with the flashcard's capacity to hold a fair number of pictures (and the current inexpensive cost of these memory cards), makes digital photography a sensibly priced medium once you get past the initial investment.

Choosing a camera

Of course, all of this organizing and storing makes sense only if you have a computer—you need to be able to plug your digital camera into it and download your photographs. When buying a digital camera, consider size and weight, cost, picture resolution (the picture-quality potential), and whether you prefer a simple point-and-shoot camera (with or without zoom) or one with more control options, like manual shutter speed and aperture (which control the amount of light allowed in through the lens). Some brands are more reliable than others, so be sure to conduct your research thoroughly before buying.

Perhaps you're not ready to give up your 35-mm camera but are interested in storing your images digitally. Most photo-processing labs will include a CD-ROM of your roll of pictures, along with the negatives and prints for an additional fee.

Compact digital cameras are perfect for "point and shoot" photographers. They are small, lightweight devices that can easily fit into a pocket, but they still give very good results.

Digital SLRs are used by serious photographers switching to working digitally. They have detachable lenses, allowing existing SLR lenses to be used with them. The downside is that they tend to be bulkier cameras, and more expensive than digital compacts.

A color printer will enable you to transform old black-and-white images. Experiment with computer software, printer settings, and paper to produce a variety of tones.

As well as flat photos and documents, you can use a scanner to photograph small objects such as jewelry, coins, and other mementos.

Using a scanner

If you are interested in digitizing your scrapbook and have a large collection of old photographs, you might consider investing in a scanner. A scanner is like a photocopy machine for photographs, documents, newspaper clippings, other ephemera, and various flat objects (such as jewelry, medals, and coins), which will either print your image directly (if the scanner is a multifunctional device with an attached printer) and/or download it onto your computer. Some printers allow you to print directly from your digital camera, without a computer, but then you need to think about how and where you might store your digital images.

Backing up

After downloading your digital images onto your computer with whatever software program you have (supplied with your digital camera), it's well worth taking the time to back them up. Who hasn't lost or heard of someone who's lost files due to a computer virus, a technical difficulty, or a power blackout? One option is to store your images on CDs, providing that your computer has a CD writer. Another option is to store them on the Internet. There are a host of websites that will allow you to store and share your digital images

for a nominal fee or even for free, such as www.kodakgallery.com and www.ofoto.com. By using these types of storage facilities, you can ensure that your precious photographs will be safe in the event of a disaster at home.

> Shop around, try as many printers as you can, and read customer reviews.

Printers

The variety and quality of printers on the market make it possible to print all your photos at home. There are inexpensive units, such as color inkjet printers, and more costly options, like color laser printers. Before you purchase one, consider the printer's compatibility with your computer, the size of prints it can produce, whether it has separate cartridges for black, cyan, yellow, and magenta (a more economical option that allows you to replace only the colors that run out), and the quality of photographs it can produce. Different printers and papers favor different tones. Some have a cold bluish hue, while others are warmer and yellow. Shop around, try as many printers as you can, and read customer reviews.

Digital Display

If you've opted to use digital photographs, try designing a scrapbook on your computer and either printing it out, publishing it on the web, or creating a CD. There are a variety of scrapbook-specific software programs on the market—some compatible with both Macs and PCs, and some only with one or the other—and you should shop around for one that best suits your abilities and needs.

Using creative software programs

Most programs come with a collection of clip art and a number of fonts and backgrounds; you simply drag and drop your images and text onto the page. Some programs have prepared page layouts, such as Art Explosion Scrapbook Factory Deluxe, which make the scrapbooking process a little easier while limiting your creativity, and some provide lists of inspirational quotations. Decide if you need a program that can crop, edit, and correct your photographs, such as Photo Express My Scrapbook, since not all scrapbook programs have this capability. You should also consider if you want to add visual variety to your presentation by turning your pictures into paintings or drawings.

If you're interested in creating your own digital pages from scratch, you might prefer working with a photo-editing program like Adobe Photoshop Elements or Jasc Paint Shop Pro, both of which come with photo-editing and repair tools and enable you to turn your photographs into artwork (drawings, etchings, colored photographs, and so on). The ACDSee Photo Manager (only compatible with PCs) offers powerful tools for organizing your photos and fixing common problems but doesn't offer the same advanced editing tools as the previous two packages.

Designing the layout

As with a nondigital scrapbook, you can layer your images, frames, artwork, and text. Different programs have different techniques to help you achieve this effect. But be careful not to clutter the page. A page full of images and text, without any

WRITER'S WORKSHOP

It's a simple process to create attractive online photo galleries in Adobe Photoshop Elements.

white space to allow for eye movement, is difficult to read. As the artist, you can control how the viewer's eye moves around the page, and it's your job to ensure that her eye doesn't fall off the page or skip items that have been improperly placed. For example, if you place a large photograph on the top-right corner of a right-side page, and a smaller image in the lower left corner, chances are your viewer's eye will go directly to the larger picture on the upper right, possibly skipping the smaller image entirely. In the West, most of us read from left to right, which is also how we tend to read pictures and pages.

When determining your layout, first decide upon your main subject—the image that will dominate the page—and arrange your other pictures, ephemera, and text so that they become supporting characters in the act and are not in direct competition with your main interest. You might want to follow the "rule of thirds": divide the page into horizontal and vertical rows of three (like a tic-tac-toe board game) and place your complementary images at any of the four corners where the lines intersect.

Once you've assembled one page, consider how it works with the facing page. You can use various design elements to spruce things up, such as blocks of color, shadows, lines, or textures. If your program doesn't come with a collection of clip art, you can purchase some online or on a CD to complement a photograph or text or to fill an empty space. Just don't overdo it. Your book will only appear consistent if you limit your range of fonts, colors, styles, and themes.

First, select File > Create > HTML Photo Gallery from the Elements menu. This will open the Adobe HTML Photo Gallery dialog box. From here, click the Add button at the bottom left to add photos to your gallery. The center area of the gallery contains four tabs, the first of which is titled Banner. This tab contains spaces for you to enter the name of your gallery.

The second tab, Thumbnails, contains options for setting the thumbnail images—small versions of your photos that can be clicked on to display the larger images. These options contain settings for the size of the thumbnail and the caption that you would like to display. You can also add the folder where you would like to save the gallery.

The third tab, Large Photos, contains options for displaying the large versions of your images. Even though these are the final images that visitors to your site will be seeing, they should still not be too big. You can change this by altering the Photo Quality setting. You can also add captions to the large images here.

Paper

Whether you're printing out your completed pages or viewing them on the computer screen, you can choose from a variety of preprinted background pages (available at craft shops) or create your own. You can either print on these papers or scan them into your computer and use them as digital backdrops. If you're interested in different textures and colors, check what paper densities your printer accepts, and experiment with rice papers, watercolor papers, and art paper. With a scanner you can create your own background pages by scanning items such as flowers, leaves, or candies. Make sure your backdrop complements and doesn't compete with the items you assemble on it.

Text

Along with digital imagery, you will need to include text. You can do this simply by choosing your font, size, and color on the computer before typing your entry into the type box (vertically or horizontally) and saving it on the page, or take a more complex approach by, for example, employing Type Mask tools, which can hollow out your letters and fill them with images from photographs or designs. Drop Shadows can add depth or emphasis to your images or text. You can accentuate the angles of your letters by beveling, or round them out by embossing. If these options don't satisfy you, you can script your letters with a drawing program or return to the scanner and create random letterlike entries by cutting text from newsprint and reassembling it on the page before scanning.

WRITER'S WORKSHOP

Most typefaces fall into two main categories: serif and sans-serif. Serifs are the small features at the end of the letter strokes, which add decoration to a typeface but also make it harder to read. Within each typeface, you can choose between roman or italic or, perhaps to open a new chapter, an elaborate treatment like embossed. Script typefaces, which mimic handwriting or calligraphy, are also highly decorative.

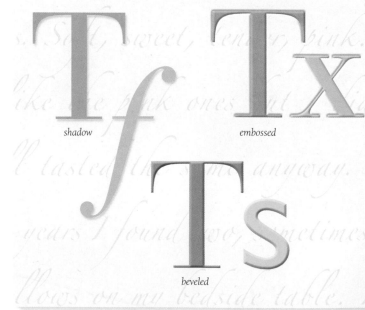

choosing your text
serif italic

choosing your text
serif

choosing your text
sans

choosing your text
script

shadow

embossed

beveled

Improving your photographs

One of the benefits of using a photo-editing program is that it allows you to repair old photographs on screen: to remove imperfections such as tears or dust specks, correct focus, improve contrast, and lighten dark areas. You can also improve photographs by cropping on screen, eliminating red-eye, flipping images (if this better serves your layout—for example, to have a picture of one individual facing the photograph of another, who is looking back at her), enlarging or downsizing, blurring undesirable details or backgrounds, making color corrections, eliminating unwanted subjects or objects, switching from color to black and white, and painting on photographs.

Experimenting

Your options are as many and varied when creating your scrapbook on the computer as they are when you choose to paste items into a book. If you think it would help your story, you might want to try making digital collages—by combining or joining images, for example. This way, you can add new subjects to old backdrops, join two or three images to form a panorama, or bring strangers together.

Remember that going digital is just another technique. Employing this technology should enhance your creative experience and help you generate new ideas. If you have a computer at home, experiment with the programs you have before investing in something new. See if a friend has a scanner or alternative software programs you can try before you decide to purchase them. Once you decide which programs best suit your needs, tap into the wealth of resources and use everything they have to offer.

Panoramas the old-fashioned way: a series of small images that capture the view section by section, joined up almost seamlessly.

This "before" image shows a photograph that's been damaged over the years with a tear in the upper right hand side. Using the Clone Stamp tool, found in Photoshop enables you to use pixels from one area of an image to replace the pixels in another part of the picture.

Another option is to use the Pattern Stamp tool to create a pattern that can be used to replace an unwanted portion of the image. The final result looks like new.

The Final Project

If yours is a digital presentation, the preceding pages have guided you toward completion of your project. Let's now return to hard copies and print. After all the labor you've invested in getting your project to this stage, it should be a pleasure to take a step back and add the finishing touches. Why not bring in a trusted friend as you do so? A fresh eye will pick up on any problems or inconsistencies that may have escaped your notice.

Last-minute revisions

By this stage you should have edited, revised, and rewritten your life-story text. The experience of writing should have helped you achieve your personal goal, whether it was to better understand or process a situation or experience, to explore new territory, or to document events in your life. Are you absolutely certain that your journey is complete? If you are satisfied with the narrative flow and visual presentation of your piece but feel you have more to say, you can include an Afterword, where you might summarize and tie off those few loose threads.

> The experience of writing should have helped you achieve your personal goal.

If a photograph now seems badly placed, reposition it or it'll be the first thing you notice when you review your project. Make a new copy of the image if moving it causes any damage—you should never use irreplaceable originals for this reason.

If any of your carefully selected photographs or ephemera now appear badly positioned or inappropriate, make revisions. (Hopefully you used a removable or repositionable adhesive.) If you have difficulty removing the item, try using a product called Un-Du (available online and from craft stores), although this won't remove permanent adhesive. If you used an expandable album, rearrange your pages if you feel that the narrative doesn't quite flow. You can also add pages if you suddenly come across lost photographs or ephemera or realize that you missed an important individual or event. It's never too late to make alterations. Since this is a life story and not a novel or any other fiction project, your presentation should first and foremost seem real. It is always worth taking the time and effort to ensure that you are happy with the overall effect you are creating.

Presentation

Whether you've just completed a memoir, a journal, or a scrapbook, you should take pride in your presentation. Be sure that your pages are free of coffee stains, creases, smeared ink, excess glue, and spelling errors. If your reader sees that you weren't interested enough in your project to care about its presentation, then why should she invest her time in reading it? After spending all of this time researching, assembling, constructing, scripting, and rewriting, why not remain a perfectionist until the end? When your story is accepted for publication or when your family and friends praise your carefully constructed scrapbook, you'll be glad you made the effort.

> When family and friends praise your carefully constructed scrapbook, you'll be glad you made the effort.

Another advantage of having used an expandable album is the freedom you now have to rearrange your pages. If something prohibits your narrative flow, see if you can remedy the situation by moving your pages around. Also don't be afraid to lose a page if it doesn't quite fit; perhaps this page can be used another time.

Whatever format you have chosen to use, make sure that the narrative of your story is clear. Is there a proper beginning, where your main characters, setting, and protagonist's plight are introduced? Are all of your characters, settings, and events relevant to your main story? If not, don't be afraid to rearrange or remove something. A scrapbook full of happy, posed photographs might not be as captivating as one that explores a more well-rounded, realistic view of your life, one that includes its ups and downs.

WRITER'S WORKSHOP

Preparing your manuscript for publication If you are submitting your work for publication, you must adhere to certain standards regarding presentation.

Your text must be double spaced with 1-inch margins all around. Print should be 12-size font and standard, like Times or Times New Roman. Always use plain white paper—nothing colored, or with graphics, patterns, or textures. Print only on one side of the paper. Number your pages and include your name in the upper-left-hand corner of the page (use the header/footer icon in your tool bar), in case your pages get separated. Don't staple your manuscript; use a paper clip, binder clip, or rubber band.

Fonts shown at actual size

12pt Times New Roman

12pt Times

name and page number

Why make things harder for yourself? Ensure the process of reading your work is as pleasant as possible by producing a spotless manuscript and following the standard conventions.

double spaced text

1" margins

Getting Published

Do you crave the validation that comes with calling yourself a published author? Attaining that holy grail demands dogged perseverance, as any established writer will tell you. Start with a realistic goal: rather than try to get a book published as a complete unknown, begin by submitting shorter pieces to literary journals.

Choosing a short piece

Have you drafted any rough short stories or essays? See if you can complete and revise them, keeping the elements of craft that are addressed in this book in mind. While you may not have as many pages over which to develop your protagonist and his plight, your main character should still lead your reader through a complete experience.

If you don't have any shorter pieces, try excerpting a chapter from your memoir. Pay attention to the fact that many chapters do not stand on their own; the reason they are chapters is because they are a part of something bigger, a piece of the whole. Whatever you submit must have a beginning, a middle, and an end. The reader must be able to identify the protagonist clearly and understand what it is that she is trying to achieve.

> Whatever you submit must have a beginning, a middle, and an end.

If excerpting a chapter isn't viable, consider writing a spin-off story that is complete in itself but is inspired by one of the themes your memoir explores or some of its characters. It's more work, but why not? Going off on a tangent like this can bring some surprising results.

Look for literary journals that publish work that is similar to yours. You should also include online publications in your research.

Literary publications

Unfortunately, for memoir and nonfiction writers most literary journals tend to focus on poetry and fiction. Some fiction/poetry journals might include one piece of nonfiction in every publication, but you have a better chance of publishing in a journal that focuses on nonfiction work. Spend some time at your local bookstore perusing its collection of literary magazines. When you look through the publications, see if they publish anything that is similar to your work. When you find a suitable publication, copy down the exact name of the journal, its editor, and the address to which you can mail submissions.

While you want to aim high, you also want to have realistic goals. You can submit your work to the leading publications, but as a new writer, the chances of having your submission accepted are slim. Begin by submitting your writing to well-known magazines and work your way down. Also keep in mind that there are now many online publications to which you can submit your work. You might begin by publishing online before venturing into the world of print.

Be persistent

The first few years of submitting work may produce standard rejection form letters or even no response at all. If you are patient and persistent, you may later begin to receive personalized rejections from the editors. Try not to take it personally. While still rejection, this is progress, since an editor has considered you worth the effort of writing a letter and the criticism offered is likely to be constructive. Keep at it: not only will your writing improve as you practice, so will your chances of publication.

Not all letters are rejections; some offer guidance. Don't give up: keep writing, keep submitting, and with luck one day you'll get a letter you'll want to frame.

WRITER'S WORKSHOP

Your cover letter Include a cover letter along with your submission. It should contain your address and that of the receiver and should be addressed to the correct editor. Make a call to check the editor's name first, if necessary.

- Paragraph 1 should introduce your work. If it's an altered excerpt from your memoir, say so. Include a brief description of your submission.

- Paragraph 2 should give details of training or education if relevant to your craft. If you have taken writing classes or attended workshops, state so here, along with details of who you studied under.

- Paragraph 3 should list your publications, if you have any. If not, include any information that connects you to the writing world, such as teaching or volunteering experience (in the field) or any contests won.

- Keep track of the publications you write to and when, so that you don't duplicate your submissions. Some publications discourage multiple submissions, but since it generally takes months to hear back, you might choose not to follow this procedure. It is very unlikely that your piece will be accepted by more than one publication simultaneously.

Searching for an Agent

The job of a literary agent is to bring writers and publishers together. Agents maintain relationships with the editors who work at publishing houses, who are generally the people that decide which books get accepted. Agents work for you (and usually earn 15 percent of your sales), which means that you should never pay an agent to read or submit your work. It's normal for agents to charge writers for the costs of mailing their work, but this is usually subtracted from the profits once the book sells. Any agent who tries to charge you a reading fee is a fraud and should be avoided.

Finding the right agent

Researching agents involves a lot more effort than researching literary magazines. If you've read any memoirs or novels that seem topically or stylistically similar to yours, find out who the writer's agent is (you'll find that the name is often listed in the acknowledgments) and contact him to find out how you should submit your work. You can also look in publications that list literary agents and agencies, but since people inevitably move around in the industry, the information you find may be out of date. The many sources available online are likely to be more reliable.

If you're looking for a literary agent in the United States, you could try Publisher's Lunch (www.publishersmarketplace.com/lunch/subscribe. html), a free weekly online publication listing book acquisitions. With a brief synopsis of the book, its genre, and the approximate price for which it was sold, the site also lists the author's agent and to whom the agent sold the work. For an additional $20 a month you can subscribe to Publisher's Marketplace (www.publishersmarketplace.com/register.shtml) and receive access to new deals, a contact database, and a larger selection of

There's nothing to stop you from sending your work directly to a publisher, but chances are it will be lost in a "slush pile" on the desk of an overworked junior. Get yourself signed up by an agent and he'll make sure the right editors read your work.

acquisitions. Some literary agencies post their contact information on the site, along with submission guidelines. In the UK *The Writers' and Artists' Yearbook* (updated annually) is the standard source of information on literary agents; their online site is found at www.writersservices.com. In Australasia try the Australian Literary Agents' Association (www.austlitagentsassoc.com.au) and the New Zealand Association of Literary Agents (www.bookcouncil.org.nz/community/organisations/nzala.html).

Submitting your work

Before you submit your work to an agent, you must be absolutely sure that it is not only finished but also it is the best piece of writing it could possibly be. It takes time to research and contact an agent, and even more time to get a response—you don't want to waste your opportunity. Normally you can submit a piece of writing to an agent only once. The only way that you can resubmit is if the agent asks that you make changes or if you rewrite the entire book.

> Give them exactly what they ask for—nothing less and not a page more.

Different agents have different submission requirements. Contact them individually to ask about their requirements if the information isn't provided on their website. Some want only a query letter (se panel on right), while others also want a synopsis and the first fifty pages of your book. Always give them exactly what they ask for—nothing less and not a page more.

Staying positive

Don't lose sight of the fact that you write to write and not to publish. If you can believe that your relationship to writing is about the act of writing itself and not about the gratification you receive upon publishing, you'll have a longer, healthier, and more gratifying connection to your craft.

Writing is a difficult business, and it can take years to publish your book; don't let this discourage you. Hopefully by this point you've established the discipline and the desire that it takes to succeed, because you'll need to maintain both while attempting to strike up a relationship with an agent. However, memoirs are published and authors find agents and publishers—and so, in time, may you!

WRITER'S WORKSHOP

Query letter This is likely to be the one and only chance you have to sell the agent your book, so do it once and do it right.

- Research your agents first. Never send the same letter to different agents. Each query letter should be addressed to a specific agent, who you've selected for a reason.

- Devote a significant amount of time to writing your query letter.

- Keep it short. A query letter should be no longer than a page.

- Keep your tone professional but also representative of your writing style.

- Describe your book briefly, explaining why it might appeal to this particular agent.

- Include information on your experience within the writing field.

- Check out some of the many sample query letters that are available online.

- As with all submissions, keep track of what you've sent to whom and when you sent it, including the type of reply you receive.

What Now?

Finishing a project is never easy. All those hours spent working are now in the past and suddenly you've got time on your hands. The empty space that it leaves can be terrifying.

Start a new project

The best way to allay any anxiety about publication and maintain momentum is to begin another project. If you've just submitted your query letter to a handful of agents, there's no point in sitting around waiting. Instead, reflect upon your recent writing experience and try to recall if there were any other ideas that came to you in the process but couldn't be addressed because they weren't relevant at the time. Are there any characters, settings, or situations that you'd like to further develop or explore? If you're not yet ready to begin another book, you may want to work on a short story or personal essay.

If you lack inspiration, revisit the many lists you've made or make some more. Go through this book again. Try keeping a journal or experimenting with free-writing exercises; you may find new ideas through this type of writing. The most important thing is not to lose the discipline that you've acquired over the duration of your life-story project. Don't let your machinery rust.

The same goes for scrapbooking; you couldn't possibly have told your entire life story in one book—and you need to keep writing. Perhaps your scrapbook focused on a particular relationship, vacation, or occasion, or maybe it was put together with one or two individuals in mind. Why not take

Ideas beget ideas. Why close the doors on your creativity now? Take what you've learned from your last project to start work on something new. If you're stuck for inspiration, start generating some lists and see what you come up with.

If you worked alone on your previous project, why not make your next a collaboration? Sound out your ideas at a writer's group, or sign up for a course to improve on a particular aspect of your craft, like dialogue. Keep writing and don't let the discipline you've learned go to waste.

your first scrapbooking experience and apply it to your second? Now that you're familiar with the medium, the process, and the tools, you're better equipped to create a second book.

> If you don't like the fit, you can keep trying until you find another medium that feels right.

If you became curious about another medium while creating your life story the first time around, now's the time to explore it. Whether it's a scrapbook, journal, memoir, personal essay, poetry, or short story, there's no harm in trying on another pair of shoes. If you don't like the fit, you can keep trying until you find another medium that feels right. Perhaps you'd like to rewrite your journal as a memoir or take an excerpt from your journal and rewrite it as a personal essay. Rewriting will only make your writing stronger. Revisiting a subject will increase your knowledge and insight.

Get support

Regardless of your medium, it helps to have support. Having deadlines to meet keeps your discipline sharp. Whether you join a writing workshop or a writer's or scrapbooker's group, others who share your desire to create will help fuel your discipline and imagination. If you like what you've done with your life-story project, do whatever it takes to keep at it—whether that's taking a writing course, setting deadlines for yourself, or working every day. And remember, it's not all about the end result. When you begin such projects, you embark on a voyage.

Publishing is a tough field, but the rewards are tremendous. Even if you're not aiming for publication, the act of completing your life story— for yourself, your friends, or family—is a major achievement and should give you a warm glow of satisfaction. Consider it a job well done and move on to your next writing project with a renewed sense of purpose and inspiration. Tell yourself that this one's going to be even better.

Resources

These titles are supplementary to those already mentioned in the book.

Further Reading

Collections

Buss, Helen M., *Mapping Our Selves: Canadian Women's Autobiography in English*, McGill-Queen's University Press, 1993

Colmer, John, *Australian Autobiography: The Personal Quest*, Oxford University Press, 1990

Conley, Cort, and Dillard, Annie (eds), *Modern American Memoirs*, HarperCollins, 1995

Gaustad, Edwin S. (ed.), *Memoirs of the Spirit: American Religious Autobiography from Jonathan Edwards to Maya Angelou*, William B. Eerdmans Publishing, 1999

Hooton, Joy W., *Stories of Herself When Young: Autobiographies of Childhood by Australian Women*, Oxford University Press, 1990

McCooey, David, *Artful Histories: Modern Australian Autobiography*, Cambridge University Press, 1996

The Penguin Book of Australian Autobiography, Penguin Books, 1987

Journals and letters

Baudelaire, Charles, *Selected Letters of Charles Baudelaire: The Conquest of Solitude*, University of Chicago Press, 1986

Guevara, Ernesto Che, *The Motorcycle Diaries: Notes on a Latin American Journey*, Ocean Press, 2003

Lorde, Audre, *The Cancer Journals: The Special Edition*, Aunt Lute Books, 1997

Nin, Anaïs, *The Diary of Anaïs Nin: Vol. 1 (1931–1934)*, Harvest Books, 1969

Plath, Sylvia, *The Unabridged Journal of Sylvia Plath*, Anchor, 2000

Woolf, Virginia, *A Writer's Diary*, Harvest/HBJ, 2003

Memoirs

Anthonioz, Geniviev de Gaulle, *The Dawn of Hope: A Memoir of Ravensbruck*, Arcade Publishing, 1999

Bauby, Jean-Dominique, *The Diving Bell and the Butterfly: A Memoir of Life in Death*, Vintage, 1998

De Beauvoir, Simone, *Memoirs of a Dutiful Daughter*, Harper, 2005

Didion, Joan, *The Year of Magical Thinking*, Knopf, 2005

Franklin, Benjamin, *The Autobiography of Benjamin Franklin*; Yale University Press, 2003

Gandhi, M. K., *Gandhi, An Autobiography: The Story of My Experiments with Truth*, Beacon Press, 1993

Gray, Francine du Plessix, *Them: A Memoir of Parents*, Penguin Press HC, 2005

Hendra, Tony, *Father Joe: The Man Who Saved My Soul*, Random House, 2005

Inez, Colette, *The Secret of M. Dulong: A Memoir*, University of Wisconsin Press, 2005

King, Martin Luther, Jr., *The Autobiography of Martin Luther King, Jr.*, Warner Books, 2001

Lupul, Manoly R., *The Politics of Multiculturalism: A Ukrainian-Canadian Memoir*, Canadian Institute of Ukrainian Study Press, 2005

Narayan, Shoba, *Monsoon Diary: A Memoir with Recipes*, Transworld, 2004

Said, Edward W., *Out of Place: A Memoir*, Vintage, 2000

Scheeres, Julia, *Jesus Land: A Memoir*, Counterpoint Press, 2005

Sebold, Alice, *Lucky*, Scribner, 1999

Stein, Gertrude, *The Autobiography of Alice B. Toklas*, Vintage, 1990

Walls, Jeannette, *The Glass Castle: A Memoir*, Scribner, 2005

Writing genres

Collom, Jack, and Noethe, Sheryl, *Poetry Everywhere*, Teachers & Writers Collaborative, New York, 2005

Gornick, Vivian, *The Situation and the Story: The Art of Personal Narrative*, Farrar, Straus and Giroux, 2002

Hampl, Patricia, *I Could Tell You Stories: Sojourns in the Land of Memory*, W. W. Norton, 2002

New, Jennifer, *Drawing From Life: The Journal as Art*, Princeton Arch, 2005

Zinsser, William, *Inventing the Truth: The Art and Craft of Memoir*, Mariner Books, 1998

Zinsser, William, *Writing About Your Life: A Journey into the Past*, Marlowe & Company, 2005

Writing style, punctuation, and grammar

Butcher, Judith, *Copy-Editing: The Cambridge Handbook for Editors, Authors, and Publishers*, Cambridge University Press, 3rd edition, 1992

The Chicago Manual of Style: The Essential Guide for Writers, Editors, and Publishers, University of Chicago Press, 15th edition, 2003

Merriam-Webster's Collegiate Dictionary, Merriam-Webster, 11th edition, 2003

Ritter, R. M., *New Hart's Rules: The Handbook of Style for Writers and Editors*, Oxford University Press, 2005

Ritter, R. M., *The New Oxford Dictionary for Writers and Editors: The Essential A–Z Guide to the Written Word*, Oxford University Press, 2nd edition, 2005

Websites

Genealogy

Ancestry
www.ancestry.com
www.ancestry.co.uk
www.ancestry.ca (Canada)
A subscription-based resource
of worldwide census, marriage,
newspaper, and various other records

Canadian Genealogy
www.canadiangenealogy.net
Canadian genealogy resources

Genealogy Canada
www.genealogycanada.com
A news service on genealogy, heritage, and history

The Genealogy Home Page
www.genhomepage.com
Links to guides, resources, lists, and libraries

Genealogylinks.net
www.genealogylinks.net/index.html
More than 40,000 genealogy links—allows you
to browse by region

Genseek—genealogy and history, Australia
www.genseek.net/index/htm
More than 900 original indexes and historical
news articles

National Library of Australia
www.nla.gov.au/oz/genelist.html
Australian family history and genealogy:
selected websites

**U.S. National Archives—genealogists/family
historians**
www.archives.gov/genealogy/
Information, events, research in genealogy
and family history

Grammar

Grammar Slammer
http://englishplus.com/grammar/
Answers all your English grammar questions online

Guide to Grammar and Writing
http://grammar.ccc.commnet.edu/grammar/
Digital handouts on grammar and English usage

Online English Grammar
www.edufind.com/english/grammar
A free online reference and guide for English grammar,
writing, punctuation, and learning

Punctuation
www.arts.uottawa.ca/writcent/hypergrammar/punct.html
A detailed look at how to use punctuation effectively
and correctly

Literary Agents

ACP: Association of Canadian Publishers
www.publishers.ca/publishing-literary-agents.htm
On getting published, distributed, and informed
about the industry

ANZ literary agents
www.doolee.com/agents
A list of Australian and New Zealand literary agents

Authorlink
www.authorlink.com
All about books, writing, and publishing: articles,
agency directory, organizations, and tips

Literary agents' e-mail addresses
www.writers-free-reference.com/agents/index.html
A free list of e-mail addresses for non-fee literary agents
in the United States, Canada, England, Australia, and
other countries

Prededitors and Editors
www.anotherealm.com/prededitors/pubagent.htm
A guide to publishers and publishing services for
serious writers

Writer's Net
www.writers.net/agents.html
Find writers, editors, agents, or publishers; allows
you to browse by country and to search by location
or topic

Memoirs

Memoir Writers
www.memoirwriters.com
Journal writing from a historical perspective

Scrapbooks

Better Homes and Gardens Scrapbooks etc.
www.bhgscrapbooksetc.com
From starting out to digital, ideas,
layouts, supplies, and techniques

Cherished Scrapbooks
www.cherishedscrapbooks.com
Stores, events, layout gallery, and news

Heritage Scrapbooks
www.crcstudio.arts.ualberta.ca/heritage
A site documenting a variety of scrapbooks on
several topics throughout the last 300 years

Organizedscrapbooks.com
http://organizedscrapbooks.com
Articles, tips, links, free printables, and
community access

Writing

American Zoetrope—home of the virtual studio
www.zoetrope.com
An online site in which you submit your writing samples
to other writers and receive feedback in exchange for
critiquing their work

AWP: Association of Writers and Writing Programs
www.awpwriter.org
Supporting writers and writing programs around
the world

Indispensable Writing Resources
www.quintcareers.com/writing
Links to all sorts of reference
material, writing labs, web
search engines, and writing-
related web search

Writing.com
www.writing.com
The online community
for writers and readers
of all interests and
skill levels

Writing-World.com
www.writing-world.com
A world of writing tips for
writers around the world

Index

Picture Credits

The publisher would like to thank the following individuals and organizations for the use of images in this book. Every effort has been made to acknowledge the pictures, however we apologize if there are any unintentional omissions.

Elaine Adler: 157, Anvil Poetry Press: 69T, **Romare Bearden Foundation**: 120–121 © Romare Bearden Foundation/DACS, London/VAGA, New York 2006, **Chronicle Books LLC**: 158L, 159TL © Nick Bantock 2004, **Corbis**: 10T/Miroslav Zazic, 12B, 21R, 31, 38, 41B, 55, 64, 70, 71, 73, 74, 77, 91, 100, 113, 117, 119, 123T, 125, 126, 133T, 141, 142, 148, 181, 182 **Cynthia Barringer**, photographer, UCDHSC College of Arts & Media: 57C, **Dial Press**, Imprint of The Bantam Dell Publishing Group, a division of Random House, Inc. 110B, **Banco de México Diego Rivera & Frida Kahlo Museums Trust**. Av. Cinco de Mayo No. 2, Col. Centro, Del. Cuauhtémoc 06059, México, D.F. © 2006/Digital Image © 2006 **The Museum of Moden Art/Scala**, Florence; 96, **Dover Press**: 131B Farrar, Straus & Giroux: 8, **Getty**: 7, 9, 12T, 28, 47, 57L, 94, 118, 129, **Granta**: 59, **Harper Perennial**: 81, 97L, **Holly Monroe**: 156, istockphoto: 15, 16, 17M, 17B, 18, 21M, 41T, 43B, 85, 86, 89, 90, 103B, 108, 180, 184T, **Jupiter Images**: 18T, 19, 22, 27, 29, 30, 34, 35T, 39, 44, 49, 52, 53, 57TR, 60, 65, 68, 72, 75, 78, 79, 83, 84, 87, 95T, 101, 106, 114, 116, 122, 124, 130, 132, 134, 135, 136, 139, 144, 145, 146, 147, 154, 177TL, **Library of Congress/Dorothea Lange** 104, **Nils Jorgensen/Rex Features**: 97R, **Ruben Joye**: Back cover TL, 76, **Michael Oreal/Visum**: 56, **Mark Morelli**: 110TR **Paper Source**: 150–151, 168B, **Picador USA**: 115, **Joyce Ravid**: 25 **Kevin Scanlon**: 112, **Karen Ulrich**: 58, 62, 158R, **JoAnn Verburg**: 99

Special Thanks

The publishers would like to thank the following people for the loan of family photographs:

Emily Bailey, Francesca Cawsey, David and Susan Earle, Katie Greenwood, Tim Harris, Rose Hopkins, Sarah Howerd, Les Hunt, Kevin Knight, Lyana Lanaway, Martyn Lanaway, Emma Lawrence, Harry Merralls, Karen Ulrich.

The publishers would also like to thank Kings Framers, Lewes, and Daisy Chain, Lewes, for the loan of props.

Lettering behind all Voices of the Masters boxes has been taken from *Toast* by Nigel Slater. Full excerpt on page 137.

Acknowledgments

Author's Acknowledgments

I'd like to thank those who taught me how to write; from my father to all the others who encouraged me to express. With the knowledge gained, I am indebted to the students who've been eager to take chances, listen, and learn. I am grateful to Carlos for his support, and to my family and friends for their inexhaustible encouragement. To the many who've participated in and helped generate my life stories, Nastrovia. And finally, thanks to Ivy Press for the opportunity and assistance in making this work.

Text Credits

Every effort has been made to trace all copyright holders and obtain permissions. The author and publishers sincerely apologize for any inadvertent errors or omissions and will be happy to correct them in future editions.

p.12: Taken from *Reading and Writing—A Personal Account* by V.S. Naipaul. Copyright © V.S. Naipaul 2000.

p.25: © *Bookforum*, Summer 2005, "Therapy, Taboo, and Perdition Eternal: Kathryn Harrison Talks With Bookforum." Reprinted by permission of Bookforum and Kathryn Harrison.

p.49: Excerpt from "The Avenue Bearing the Initial of Christ into the New World" from *What a Kingdom It Was: Poems by Galway Kinnell*. Copyright © 1960, renewed 1988 by Galway Kinnell. Reprinted by permission of Houghton Mifflin Company. All rights reserved.

pp.53, 77: Taken from *Childhood* by Nathalie Sarraute, published by George Braziller, 1984.

p.59: Excerpt from *My Life in Orange*, copyright © 2004 by Tim Guest, reprinted by permission of Harcourt, Inc.

p.69: "A Dream of Mountaineering" by Po Chu-I, translated by Arthur Waley, taken from *Poems of Sleep and Dreams*, edited by Peter Washington, published by Everyman's Library Pocket Books, 2004.

p.73: Selection (Dalai Lama writes about his mother in Tibet) from *Freedom in Exile: The Autobiography of the Dalai Lama* by Tenzin Gyatso. Copyright © 1990 by Tenzin Gyatso, His Holiness, The Fourteenth Dalai Lama of Tibet. Reprinted by permission of HarperCollins Publishers.

p.91: Reprinted from *The Diary of Frida Kahlo: An Intimate Self-Portrait* by Sigrid Sangl. Published by Harry N. Abrams, Inc., New York. All rights reserved.

p.97: Excerpt from *Autobiography of a Face* by Lucy Grealy. Copyright © 1994 by Lucy Grealy. Reprinted by permission of Houghton Mifflin Company. All rights reserved.

p.97: From *An Evil Cradling: The Five-Year Ordeal of a Hostage* by Brian Keenan, copyright © 1992 Brian Keenan. Used by permission of Viking Penguin, a division of Penguin Group (USA) Inc.

p.99: "Seven Invisible Strings," copyright 2005 by Jim Moore. Reprinted from *Lightning at Dinner*, with the permission of Graywolf Press, Saint Paul, Minnesota.

p.107: Reprinted with the permission of Scribner, an imprint of Simon & Schuster Adult Publishing Group, from *Angela's Ashes* by Frank McCourt. Copyright © 1996 by Frank McCourt.

p.110: From *Drinking: A Love Story* by Caroline Knapp, copyright ©1995 by Caroline Knapp. Used by permission of The Dial Press/Dell Publishing, a division of Random House, Inc.

p.119: From *Up in the Old Hotel* by Joseph Mitchell, copyright © 1992 by Joseph Mitchell. Used by permission of Pantheon Books, a division of Random House, Inc.

p.119: From *The Diary of a Young Girl: The Definitive Edition* by Anne Frank. Otto H. Frank and Mirjam Pessler, Editors, translated by Susan Massotty. [For US] copyright © 1995 by Doubleday, a division of Random House, Inc. Used by permission of Doubleday, a division of Random House, Inc. [For UK] copyright © The Anne Frank-Fonds, Basle, Switzerland, 1991. English translation copyright © Doubleday, a division of Bantam Doubleday Dell Publishing Group, Inc., 1995.

p.123: Excerpts from Vladimir Nabokov's *Speak, Memory: An Autobiography Revisited* are reprinted here by arrangement with the Estate of Vladimir Nabokov. All rights reserved.

p.125: [For US] From *The Autobiography of Malcolm X* by Malcolm X and Alex Haley, copyright © 1964 by Alex Haley and Malcolm X. Copyright © 1965 by Alex Haley and Betty Shabazz. Used by permission of Random House, Inc. [For UK] From *The Autobiography of Malcolm X*, published by Hutchinson. Reprinted by permission of The Random House Group Ltd.

p.133: [For US] From *In Search of Lost Time, Vol. 6, Time Regained* by Marcel Proust, translated by Moncrieff & Kimartin rev. by D. J. Enright, copyright © 1981 by Chatto & Windus and Random House Inc. Revisions to the translation copyright © 1992 by D. J. Enright. Used by permission of Modern Library, a division of Random House, Inc. [For UK] From *In Search of Lost Time* by Marcel Proust, published by Chatto & Windus. Reprinted by permission of The Random House Group Ltd.

p.135: [For US] From *Virginia Woolf* by Nigel Nicolson, copyright © 2000 by Nigel Nicolson. Used by permission of Viking Penguin, a division of Penguin Group (USA) Inc. [For UK] From Virginia Woolf by Nigel Nicolson, published by Weidenfeld & Nicolson, an imprint of The Orion Publishing Group.

p.137: From *Toast: The Story of a Boy's Hunger* by Nigel Slater, copyright © 2003 by Nigel Slater. [For US] Used by permission of Gotham Books, an imprint of Penguin Group (USA) Inc. [For UK] © Nigel Slater 2003.